FULL CIRCLE

A MEMOIR

PAMELA LOMBANA

Wordfall Publishing

FULLCIRCLE

For more information, contact
pamelalombanaauthor@gmail.com
or visit the publisher's website at
www.wordfallpublishing.com.

Writing Coach: Fern Brady
Copyediting: D Tinker Editing
Formatting: Manon Lavoie
Cover Design: Verstandt

ISBN: 978-1-7342347-0-1

Library of Congress Control Number: 2019918766

Houston, TX

11 10 9 8 7 6 5 4 3 2

Dedication

To my mother, who always believed in me.
To my beloved children — Christina, Nicholas, and Natalia —
whom I love and who gave me a reason to live.

To my brother, Juan, and my sister by marriage, Elsa. To my
sisters, Cynthia and Elizabeth, who have always loved me,
even when life put distance between us.

To my dearest husband, Mark, who taught me how to love
and trust again.

To my beloved God:
You knew me before I was born, you've always been at my
side, you carried me when I couldn't walk, and you've
surrounded me with grace and love.

CONTENTS

PREFACE

I started writing this book many years ago when I was still married. It began as my own personal diary and as letters to communicate with my husband that ended up shredded, torn, or swallowed. Then, with the passage of time, I wrote letters to my children. Thoughts, feelings, and words that couldn't be expressed through voice and sound flowed easily onto paper. Writing was my outlet. The words that poured onto paper gave me clarity and insight.

Still, it was eleven years after I made the decision to ask for a divorce and start a new life that a book truly began to take shape.

I wrote this book for my children. I wanted them to understand what we lived so that they wouldn't repeat the cycle of abuse or alcohol in their lives. Domestic abuse does not discriminate; it can happen to anyone. The National Domestic Violence Hotline describes abuse as "a pattern of behaviors used by one partner to maintain power and control over another partner." The National Institutes of Health has classified "problem drinking that becomes severe" as "'alcohol use disorder' or AUD. AUD is a chronic relapsing brain disease characterized by compulsive alcohol use, loss of control over alcohol intake, and a negative emotional state when not using."

When my oldest daughter, Christina, learned I had signed up for a writer's workshop, she called me. "Mom, I wrote the introduction to your book."

"Really? When will I see it?" I asked, full of curiosity.

"I just sent it to your email, Mom. I want you to use it! It's our story," she said, before hanging up.

I opened my computer and started reading. I smiled at the incredible insight she had as a twenty-five-year-old. Her input motivated me to tell our story.

INTRODUCTION
OUR STORY—MAMI'S BOOK

This is my mom's story. It is also my story. And my siblings' stories. It is all our stories. It is a story of alcoholism, illness, fear, hatred, escape, love, and ultimately, forgiveness and death.

My father was not a good father. I do not believe that you can be a bad husband and a good father; the two roles go hand in hand, and part of being a good father is giving your children an example of true love. My dad adored my mom, but it wasn't enough for him. He always had to have more: more money, more women, more love, more whiskey. Always more. Practicing moderation was not his strong suit, and it ultimately killed him.

Ever since I can remember, I was just a little afraid of my dad. My mom tells a story that took place early on in their marriage: One time, my father came home to a mess; there were toys all over the floor. We were two kids under two, and I'm sure it wasn't easy keeping up with us. He started yelling at her, and I, at eighteen months, came up to him and started saying, "No, no, no, Papi, no." However, I don't remember that. I never felt that brave, not enough to stand up to him again—at least, not until many, many years later.

In my first memory of my dad, I was about three years old and crying. I don't really know why; possibly, it was one of his practical jokes that had seemed funny to everyone except the victim of the joke, or perhaps he had raised his voice at me and I got scared.

My dad was not a bad man, but he was a tormented one. All his life, he carried demons of the abuse he suffered at the hands of my grandmother. He never laid a finger on us because, in his eyes, then he, too, would have been the abuser. He could be the kindest, funniest person, but he could also be the most terrifying—all within a matter of minutes. He was mercurial and volatile. You could never quite be sure when the switch would flip, and it was incredibly stressful, particularly for a young child.

There are many people who remember my dad as a saint or as the life of the party—always ready to lend money or tell a joke. I also remember my dad that way, but he was so much more complex than most people ever knew.

Life is not just black and white; humans are not simply good or evil. In every person, there is the capacity for good and the capacity for evil. Our lives are defined by the choices we make. Some decisions are more harmless, like choosing cars or choosing a job, but other choices can start you down a path toward self destruction.

My dad didn't start down that path consciously. I know he had no intention of hurting the people he loved, of pushing away everyone who cared about him, or finally, of killing his body. He wanted to be a father and husband with the perfect family, but he also wanted to be the "fun" friend, the "rich" friend, the brilliant playboy to whom young boys looked up.

These were only a few of the many complex pieces that made up my dad. Ultimately, he made many, many choices that led him further and further away from the family man and closer to his young death.

This is the story of how we coped, how we survived, and how we were transformed.

Christina Lombana

January 23, 2016

THE PRISONER
FALL 2004

Looking out the kitchen window, I feel life passing me by. I turn around and take in the sparkling black granite kitchen counters, the Italian-tile flooring, and the large double-paned windows of this house. Sitting on two acres of land, it is beautiful, yet I am trapped. I'm a bird in a gilded cage, and the key has been lost. I scream, but no one can hear me. My spirit has been crushed; I'm suffocating.

I close my eyes and think of confined animals. I begin to understand the pacing I've seen them do at the zoo, their eyes lifeless. They are prisoners. They will never be out in the wilderness, roaming and running freely.

As I look around, I realize this is not the life I want to live. So what keeps me here? The children? Him? Our wedding vows? Paralyzing fear?

No answer comes. I close my eyes and pray: *Dear God, I'm dying. Please help me live until my youngest daughter, Natalia, graduates from high school.* It is a simple, desperate prayer, lifted to heaven.

I open my eyes. My chest is tight. I'm a prisoner.

I open my arms. I want to fly into the sky — wings spread out, the wind on my face, the sun warming me up. Finally free to live. I speak the words that have been in my heart for years.

"I have a choice to change my life. I have to get out."

I say it. I hear it. I know the decision I need to make. It is time.

1

COLOMBIA

I grew up in Medellín, Colombia, the land of orchids, coffee, music, and mountains. Medellín is called the City of the Eternal Spring, and it holds one of the largest flower festivals in the world. It is the second largest city in Colombia and is located in a central region of the Andes Mountains.

My childhood was carefree. I lived in the moment. There was no thought of the past and definitely no thoughts as to the future.

My father was Colombian. He was born and raised in Cartago, a farming community. His father and grandfather both loved the land, and agriculture was their life. Their ancestry went back to the Basque region in Spain.

My father attended Louisiana State University in Baton Rouge to study agricultural engineering in the early 1950s. My mother, a native of Baton Rouge, was a nursing student at Our Lady of the Lake Regional Medical Center. They met in a chemistry class. He fell in love with the beautiful blonde, and she with the handsome tanned foreigner. It seemed a match made in heaven.

They courted for two years, got engaged, and were married as soon as my mother had graduated. She had dreams of moving to Colombia and living an exotic life. She didn't understand the social unrest within Colombia and how different it would be to live in an underdeveloped country in the fifties. America was a vibrant society; in Colombia, there was political turmoil.

Nevertheless, they married and moved to Cartago, a rural farming community. My mother was a city girl trying to adapt to a new life. Her world closed in. Her dreams slowly shattered. Her joy in life was replaced by a need to survive.

In 1961, my parents started their family with the birth of my brother, Juan. I followed in 1963, Cynthia in 1966, and Elizabeth in 1967. Before Elizabeth was born, they moved from Cartago to Medellín. A severe drought had caused the crops to fail for two consecutive years. My father couldn't recover financially and had to look for new work.

While in Cartago, the country setting had provided a sense of freedom for me as a child. Our house there had consisted of adobe walls and terracotta tile, with a hay roof that allowed the breeze to blow through. Outside, I would run after the clucking chickens that dotted the property. Juan and I would climb the tractors parked out in front of the house and swing in colored hammocks hanging from the wooden beams of the porch in the evenings. Looking out the front windows, I could see fields of golden wheat and light-brown rice shooting up toward the sky. When it was windy, they would appear to dance softly.

When the drought came, the fields turned bare and dry, the ground harsh and rocky. The chickens slowly disappeared. There was no more work, and the laborers were dismissed one by one, leaving the tractors to rust away, unused.

The move to Medellín meant transitioning from a small farming community to a city with traffic, large neighborhoods, and reduced space. The new house was white and had a small concrete yard in the back, where all the clothes were washed by hand in a basin and hung up to dry. It was a move from spending our days outside to spending most of our time indoors.

For my mother, it was a relief; she loved the city. My father found a job at a bank appraising agricultural farms and ranches. It took him all over Colombia, and he would return from his trips with bags of fruit and animals.

The moment my father arrived home from his trips, we would eagerly run up to him to kiss and hug him. Then we would start asking, "Papi, Papi, what did you bring us this time?"

One day he returned, I squealed joyfully, "Papi, what are you hiding? What's under the sheet?"

"Today, I brought something really special and very, very colorful." He smiled and laughed as we excitedly clapped our hands, jumping around the room.

"Papi, what is it?" we all screamed, full of curiosity.

"I brought a toucan, and it has the most colorful bill of any I've seen." He smiled and pulled the sheet off the cage he held to show us the bird within it.

"It's beautiful! Is it ours to keep?" I asked in awe as I looked at the magnificent bird, then glanced at my father.

"Yes, but we have to be gentle. We don't want to scare him." He opened the cage and placed the bird on his arm. The toucan would live with us for many years.

After another trip, my father brought back parrots that learned to repeat words we taught them. They loved to say: "*Lorito quiere cacao. Bobo, loco,* hello." He brought home turtles, chickens, and ducks. All of these lived in the backyard until they died or became dinner.

For Thanksgiving, my father would always bring home a live turkey. He and my brother would give the turkeys rum until the birds started tipping over, and then they would twist the turkeys' necks to kill them. After that, plucking their feathers was a family affair.

We also had a collie named Tania, which was my mother's dog. After the dog died, my father bought my mother an Irish setter she named Rocky. One day, Rocky ran out of the garage after a car, which came to a sudden stop. The resulting impact killed Rocky instantly.

We were all so grief-stricken over Rocky's death that my father thought he could ease our pain by having him embalmed.

"Sybil, children, I have a surprise for you. Come to the living room." His excited voice drew us to the living room, where he stood next to a big object covered with a blanket.

"Papi, Papi what is it?" my sisters asked eagerly before he pulled the blanket off.

"It's Rocky," he answered proudly. "He can now be with us in the living room everyday."

"Mario, you had him embalmed? He doesn't even resemble him." My mother had tears in her eyes.

"It's a little creepy, Papi. We don't want a dead dog. We loved him alive, not like this," Juan said, trying to help our father understand why it wasn't cool to have an embalmed dog in the house.

My sisters and I were speechless. My father had been so happy when he brought the embalmed Rocky home, but we didn't want a dog we couldn't play with. Rocky was shortly removed from the house.

My father was a dreamer. He made life fun for us kids, but difficult for his wife. He loved to read poetry. Pablo Neruda, the Nobel Prize–winning Chilean, was his favorite poet. My dad knew his poems by heart and would recite them at night. He particularly loved *Twenty Love Poems and a Song of Despair*. Others of his favorite writers included Gabriel García Márquez and Agatha Christie. He tried many ventures and businesses throughout his life, but most failed. My mother quickly learned that she needed to support the family, as she could never count on him.

As a child, I remember my mother working and studying all the time. She was called "La Gringa" at the Universidad de Antioquia, where she taught psychiatric nursing. It was a term with many connotations. If the people were happy with

American policies and ideas, it was a term of endearment. If they were angry with America's effect on their country, it became a hateful term.

One night, when I was ten, she came home crying and scared. It was around seven o'clock in the evening, and the sky was dusky. When I heard my mom's voice, I sat on the stairway leading up to the second floor, where I could hear and not be seen, hidden by a half wall. My parents both stood in the middle of the living room, and I could tell Mom was very agitated.

"Mario, they are striking again. They're targeting all American teachers. They even burned a car on campus today. The students are blocking the streets to the university, and classes have stopped. I was afraid just to leave my office." Mom's voice quivered, and she broke down in tears.

I could hear her pacing. I imagined she was probably waving her arms in the air. I took a quick glance, trying not to get caught, and I saw stress in my dad's face. He knew this was a frequent occurrence and that, after the strike, everything would return to normal.

"You can't be afraid. There will always be strikes," my father said calmly, trying to reassure her. "It is the only way for them to get the government's attention. They will strike for a few days, the university will close, and then it will reopen." He drew her into his arms.

"It's different this time," she said as he held her, her hands splaying against his chest. "The students have posted graffiti signs across campus that say, 'Gringos, go back to your country! We don't want Americans in our universities.' Please," she begged, tears running down her face, "let's just move to the States. I'm afraid, and I know you could get a job at LSU."

Releasing her, my father moved to the doorway. "No, I will never move back. This is my country. This is my children's country. This is home." The sternness in his voice brooked no argument.

His word was final. Each time the subject was brought up, he refused to discuss it.

There were fights about money. The most important ones concerned the key to the locked desk, where he kept the financial information. His secrecy made her fearful. She never knew what their situation really was. He was the man; he managed the money. Mom's salary went to him. My parents lived paycheck to paycheck. My father even chose not to pay taxes for several years.

He struggled financially, but we never understood this as kids. There was always just tension, bills to be paid, and stress between my parents. When the screaming started, I went to my room, my refuge. There, I would think of all the things I loved about my life: my school, swim team, and my friends. I loved my father and couldn't understand why my mother had to argue with him; I always took his side. I was ten years old, and I wanted Mom to love Colombia the way I did.

One summer, when I was twelve, my mother won a significant amount of money in a raffle. My father was delighted and took us on a month-long road trip through Ecuador. We loved the vacation, but when we got back, the fights resumed. I still didn't understand. We had had so much fun, so why was my mother upset that the money had been used on the vacation?

A shadow was falling upon our family; there was a darkness engulfing us. As it progressed, my siblings and I tried to spend weekends with friends to avoid being at home.

When Juan graduated from high school, he was admitted to the university to study dentistry in Medellín. I vividly remember how difficult his first year in dental school was for me. Up to that point in our lives, we'd shared the same friends, loved the same music, and enjoyed being together. During his first semester in college, he made new friends, and we had less time together. Life was putting distance between us. And the next year, in 1981, I left the country. The rest of the family would slowly join me over the next couple of years.

I applied to LSU in 1980, my senior year of high school. It was a dream I had had since I was a child, when I would listen to my parents' stories of their alma mater. The day I got my acceptance letter, I cried for joy.

My mother was in the living room sorting the mail when she saw the white eight-by-eleven envelope from LSU. She called out my name several times.

"Pamela, Pamela! You have mail."

I was sitting on my bed, reading, when I heard her voice.

"Don't open it! I'm coming down!" I screamed excitedly.

I jumped off the bed and ran downstairs, where I saw her holding the envelope. She smiled and handed it to me. Her blue eyes sparkled, as if she already knew what it said.

I turned it over and saw the LSU return address. It felt smooth. I smelled it, as if trying to grasp the scent of the airplane it had arrived on. Holding it close to my heart, I took a breath before tearing it open. Expectation hung heavily in the air. A thought went through my mind: *This determines if I stay or if I go; please, please, let it be my admission.*

As soon as opened it, I began to scream excitedly, jumping and hugging my mother. "Papi, Juan, Cynthia, Elizabeth, I've been accepted! I've been accepted to LSU!"

Everyone, except my dad, came to the living room, already dressed in their pajamas. We all hugged. My sisters were crying in joy.

"Pamelita, we are happy for you, but we don't want you to go so far away," said Elizabeth.

"It's your dream!" my brother said with a big smile. "It's exciting."

"Where's Papi?" I asked, looking around.

Mom looked at me. After a moment of silence, she spoke, her voice laced with sadness. "He's not here right now. He'll be home later."

"I'm going to LSU. It's everything I've dreamed of," I screamed happily. I reread the letter and smiled as I tried to contain my joy. Everyone settled onto the brown sofas around coffee table. "I'll go to college and come back to Colombia during the summers. I need to talk to dad about the money for tuition and the dorm. He has it set aside. I can't wait to graduate from high school so I can start studying psychology. This is wonderful!"

"I think we need to talk," my mother said then, giving my siblings a look. They understood and got up to go. I was still smiling, giddy; it felt like nothing could take that moment of joy away.

Coming to sit beside me, Mom hugged me for a long moment.

"I'm so happy you'll be studying at LSU. I wish we could all go and stay there. Things are very difficult here at home right now. Your dad and I might get divorced." Tears filled her eyes.

I felt nauseated then, and a knot formed in my stomach. I didn't have the voice or the courage to tell Mom I had met the other woman the week before. I just cried and held the envelope close to my heart.

The week before, my dad had picked me up in our white 1972 Simca, with its blue cloth seats. It was a small car, perfect for a family of four adults or two adults and four small children, though we had almost outgrown it as a family. I had stayed at school to practice for graduation, so my sisters weren't with me. Dad had told me that morning that we would be doing something special after school. We both loved rum-raisin ice cream, so I had thought we would be going to the ice cream shop or maybe to Mimo's, the popular ice cream store that had recently opened. It was going to be our special time together.

As the car approached, I noticed he was laughing and talking with a woman who sat in the front seat. *Who is she? Why is she in my seat? He's supposed to pick me up to spend time with me.* The jealous thoughts raced through my mind.

The car finally came to a stop, and I opened the back door to get in. A surge of anger ran up my spine. It was the same sensation I had felt as a child when I would use foul language and my mouth would be washed with soap. As I settled in, I breathed deeply, tucking the anger away. I continued to take deep breaths until I could speak. My dad tried to engage me in conversation, but something didn't feel right.

"Pamelita, this is Marta; we work together. I wanted you to meet her," he had said as I climbed in.

"Hi," I said suspiciously, eyeing her from head to toe and refusing to smile. I had never even heard of her. *How long had she been around?* I asked myself silently, knowing I would never really get an answer.

"I've heard a lot about everything you like to do. Your father is always talking about his children. I'm so happy we're finally meeting." She gave me a big smile and put her hand gently on my dad's knee, caressing it and looking at me defiantly. She reminded me of a dog marking its territory.

"I've been telling her about things you like: tennis, swimming, and painting. She likes them too," Dad said as he turned around in his seat. He smiled and made eye contact with me as I buckled my seatbelt. I held his gaze but still refused to smile.

He was excited. Enthralled by her. He couldn't stop talking and trying to engage me in conversation.

"Good," I replied as I looked out the window. He talked, and I continued to answer with monosyllables. In my head, a voice screamed, *No, no, no, this is not happening. He likes her. No. I know you are not happily married, but I don't want to meet your girlfriend!*

I eventually stopped answering his questions. When he dropped me off at the house, I slammed the door without saying goodbye and ran up to my bedroom. I locked the door, looked around at my desk, my single bed with its floral print, and my animal posters that hung on the wall. This was my haven, but I was angry. I grabbed my pillow and started hitting the wall and screaming.

"I hate her! How can he do this right now? I hate her. How can he bring his girlfriend when I'm leaving? I hate her!" I continued until I collapsed on the bed crying, and I was eventually wrapped in sleep.

I had always thought there would be no problem paying for college. My father had promised that there was money set aside, and I had believed him. But when the moment came, there wasn't even money for airline tickets, let alone for my education. My maternal grandparents had to pay my airfare into the States.

During my last week in Colombia, I tried to eat everything I loved: arepas, empanadas, *ajiaco*, and *bandeja paisa*. I saw all my friends and said goodbye with hugs and tears. I was the first one to leave our family home. There was excitement combined with sadness.

"I'm leaving, but I'll be coming back to work," I told everyone I saw during that last week. "I'm just going there to study. This is my country; I will be back."

My entire family saw me off at the airport. We all shed tears, but I was ready for all my dreams to come true.

COLLEGE

When I arrived in Baton Rouge, I was still anxiously waiting for a check to arrive from my father so I could pay tuition for my first semester. It never did. My grandmother helped me apply for loans and grants, and I got a job in the school cafeteria. It was the first time in my life that I had ever felt like my father had lied to me. I felt betrayed. How much easier it would have been if he had just told me the truth. A simple sentence would have sufficed: "There is no money for college. You will have to work and apply for scholarships, but this is possible in the States." I believe in my heart that I would have understood.

I thought about my mother and her fights with him. Maybe she had been right. Mother had never known anything about the finances at home, not even her own since she gave him her full check. Anytime she questioned him about whether they had enough money to do things, they ended up in an argument.

After my freshmen year of college, my sisters, Elizabeth and Cynthia, who were fourteen and fifteen respectively, moved to Oklahoma to live with my Aunt Diane and Uncle Tom. It was an act of love by our family in Oklahoma. My parents were separating at the time, and my mother couldn't afford to keep my sisters in Colombia. My mother would move after my sophomore year and file for divorce the following year in Baton Rouge.

My first six months of college were a culture shock. I experienced frequent headaches due to listening to English all day and translating it in my mind. I was homesick. I wanted to speak Spanish and eat Colombian food. I dreamed of going back home, yet economically, it was impossible.

Dorm life was another surprise for me. My roommate, Kim, would spend mornings in our dorm watching soap operas and the show *Love Boat*. The dorm room was sparkling white and had two single beds lined up against the walls and divided by a nightstand. I had moved in with a lilac comforter, a towel, and a suitcase of clothes, just enough to fill our small closet. She had a blue flowery comforter, some posters of TV stars, and a bulletin board filled with pictures from her high school events.

Our goals in life and our upbringings were completely different. I had a strong accent and struggled to understand the American way of life. I had seen the movie *Animal House* before leaving Colombia, and I wasn't sure what was fiction and what was true about life in the States. Fraternity parties scared me, based on what I'd seen in the movie.

Kim was a tall, beautiful blonde. She would wake up at five in the morning to fix her hair. I still remember one of the first conversations we had that year.

"Kim, what are you majoring in?" I asked excitedly, trying to become friends. I'd sat down on my bed and had propped my head and back against the cold white wall.

"I want an MRS Degree," she said, smiling and swinging her blonde hair around from side to side.

"What type of job can you get with an MRS degree?"

"You don't know what that means?" Kim asked. She lifted an arrogant eyebrow as she turned to look at me. I could see the contempt in her clear blue eyes.

"No, I don't," I whispered, embarrassed by my lack of

knowledge concerning something that seemed so mundane and simple.

"I want to stay home and have babies. I don't want to work." She returned her gaze to the mirror. "I want to find a husband in college." A look of fierce determination came over her face.

I smiled and remained silent. The conversation was finished. I wanted a college degree. My mother had worked all her life. I dreamed about marriage, but more than anything at that point in my life, I wanted a career. I was hungry for knowledge.

My body really saw a change too. I gained twenty-five pounds my first year of college. During my sophomore year, my brother came to Baton Rouge for Christmas. Excited to pick him up at the airport, I was waiting outside the gate when he arrived. However, he passed right by without recognizing me.

I called out, "Juan, Juan, I'm here," as I ran to hug him, smiling and excited.

"Pamelita, I didn't recognize you. *Estás gordita.* What have you been eating?" He laughed as he embraced me.

"Juan, it's the dorm food. Most students gain fifteen pounds, but I gained thirty! The food in the cafeteria is delicious, but I'm working on trying to lose weight. I've really missed you." I smiled, holding onto his arm.

"I'm happy to see you too. Work on the weight. It isn't good for you, and if you don't lose it now, it'll be harder to later," he said gently, smiling as we walked toward the baggage claim.

Despite all the difficulties, college life gave me a freedom I loved. The ability to have classes at different times of the day was amazing. I remember talking to the counselor and being in awe.

"You need fifteen credits your first semester," the freshman college counselor said encouragingly as I tried to decipher orientation. "So let's look at how you can arrange the classes you need. These classes are held on Mondays, Wednesdays, and

Fridays, while these are on Tuesdays and Thursdays. You can have some long days and some short days. Plan your classes around open time slots so you can have breaks in between."

"You mean, it's not an eight in the morning to four in the afternoon schedule? I don't have to have early classes?" I was amazed by how much flexibility college allowed.

The counselor smiled. "You can start classes at seven in the morning or at noon, and you can spread them out. You're taking fifteen hours, so it's going to be a busy schedule. All this free time right now won't seem like enough in one month."

For the next four years, I went to classes and lectures, listened to fascinating professors, and rode my bike around campus.

I had gone to the American school in Medellín with the same sixty students from kindergarten through twelfth grade. Year after year, I had seen the same people and sat in all the classrooms of the school. Columbus School was surrounded by trees and open spaces, away from the noise of the city.

The first time I set foot on the LSU campus, I was struck by its size, its beautiful landscape, and the peaceful sounds of the Mississippi River. Large magnolia trees with white blossoming flowers and thick green leaves surrounded me. The air was hot and humid most of the year, but I didn't mind. In the spring and fall, I would sit in the middle of the LSU open green quadrangle, reading, studying, and watching other students play Frisbee or sunbathe. I also loved the school colors—gold and purple—and the mascot, Mike the Tiger.

I applied for jobs on campus and was thrilled to get one in the cafeteria. It paid above minimum wage at five dollars an hour. I was ecstatic. Life couldn't be better! The day I got my first paycheck, I held it close, opened the envelope excitedly, and smiled at the fifty-dollar check. I knew right then that nothing would ever stop me from getting an education. I was rich!

LSU helped me fall in love with America. The university radiated life and energy. Off campus, my favorite pastime was walking into pharmacies. I vividly remember their unique clean, crisp smell. They were full of products that weren't necessarily medicine. They had toys and gadgets. The pharmacies were places I could buy all the souvenirs I would need when I returned, whenever that might be. It was a happy time in my life.

In my junior year of college, my mother moved to Baton Rouge from Colombia, and my sisters joined her from Oklahoma. When I saw her, I was struck by how she had aged. She was five foot one with fair skin, light golden hair, and blue eyes, but she had become skin and bones. Her laughter was gone, and her heart was broken. She would regain her laughter years later with her grandchildren, but I felt her loss then in my heart. I was kind to her. Years of anger had melted away.

I often thought of my father, but after my mother moved to the States, we lost contact with him. Our house had been sold, our phone disconnected. He changed jobs and moved around Colombia several times, eventually leaving no trace of where he was.

For years to come, it would haunt me that he had disappeared completely from our lives when my mom moved to the States. We missed our father, though we never talked about him. We all felt he had abandoned us when he divorced our mom. We didn't know where he was or why there was silence from him. It was a hole that would remain in our hearts for nine years.

I left dorm life and the convenience of living on campus to move in with my mother and my sisters. We found a two-bedroom apartment that was affordable, though we didn't realize it was located in a sketchy neighborhood. My mom had looked at the place during the day but had never seen it at night or met the people that lived there. She signed a one-year lease.

Soon after we moved in, we witnessed cars being broken into frequently, domestic violence incidents in the parking lot, and police cars coming to the apartment complex regularly. My sisters and I would peek through the window blinds and make sure our lights were off every time we heard the police sirens. We had grown up in a calm neighborhood, so the local crime sent chills down our spines.

"Elizabeth, Cynthia, hurry! Come and see what's going on in the parking lot!" I screamed one day after hearing the sirens.

"Did you see that?" Elizabeth said, crying. "He's drunk and hitting her! She's screaming, and the cops are coming. How long do we have to stay here? This is scary. There are always problems here. It's not safe. I hate this life."

I held her in my arms. "We can't move right now. We can't afford to move until the lease is up. I hate it too, but we need to make the best of it right now."

It was a difficult time for my mother. She worked two jobs to cover our expenses. We all had part-time jobs, but she had the biggest load. She worked from seven in the morning to three in the afternoon at one hospital and then went to another for the three-to-eleven shift. At night, she walked in exhausted, yet I never remember her complaining.

One night, she walked in at 11:45 p.m., sat on the couch, and started crying.

"Mom, are you okay?" I asked. "Can I get you a peanut butter sandwich?" She loved peanut butter. It had been the only thing she would ask her American friends to bring back from the States when she lived in Colombia.

"Yes, and a glass of milk. I'm tired today. The adolescents were acting out in the psychiatric unit. They had to call a lockdown, and no one was allowed to leave their rooms. It only made them angrier." She ate her sandwich, took off her shoes, laid down on the beige sofa, and fell asleep within moments.

"Mom, do you regret coming back to the States? Do you miss Colombia?" I asked one weekend when the two of us were home alone.

She turned around and smiled slowly. Her blue eyes sparkle with a twinkle. "This was my dream, to come back to my country with my family, but not in this way. I'm fifty years old, divorced, and without a penny. I left twenty-five years ago, and it was a different country then. I missed the sixties, the seventies, and the Beatles. It has been difficult to adjust. I am a stranger in my own land. I need to work to support myself and help you all as much as I can. I just have to do it. Someday, when you're a mother, you'll understand the sacrifices a mother gives for her children."

"I'm sorry it's so hard, Mom," I said, lowering my voice and giving her a hug.

I was a microbiology premed major. During the week, I worked at the school cafeteria at lunch time. In the evenings, I worked in the catering department of the university. On weekends, I got a night-shift job as a psychology tech at a psychiatric hospital. We all knew our financial situation was tight. At home, we all shared chores; Elizabeth and I took turns cooking dinner.

"Cynthia, are you cooking or cleaning dishes?" I'd ask every day, even though I already knew the answer.

"I hate cooking! If you all want to eat white rice, then I'll cook. Can we eat something other than beans today?"

"You can fix yourself a peanut butter sandwich. You can't be picky if you're not cooking. The meal today is red beans and rice." I laughed.

We shopped for clothes at Fashion Gal, a small discount clothing store. On weekends, we would walk to the 7-Eleven and rent a VCR to watch movies.

18

"Monita, you can't go out until you set up our VCR so we can see movies," Cynthia would tell Elizabeth every Friday evening, especially if there was a football game at the high school.

"You and Pamelita need to learn how to do it!" Elizabeth would respond, frustrated. "You are never going to learn if I'm always the one doing it." Then she would try to teach us again. "Look at the back of the TV. Red cable with red cable, yellow with yellow. Then you switch the settings on the device. Does that make sense?"

"No, it doesn't make sense to me," Cynthia would respond with a serious look on her face.

"Pamelita, Cynthia, what's going to happen if I have a date?" Elizabeth would look at us stubbornly.

"Well, your date would have to wait until the VCR is installed. Or we could all go on the date with you," I would say triumphantly, and the three of us would start laughing together.

One day, we were shopping for clothes at the discount store when Elizabeth turned to face me. "Pamelita, are we poor?"

"Monita, how can we be poor if we have each other? We just have to work and study!" I picked some shirts from the rack to try on, then looked up at her. "It's common to work while going to school in the States. We wouldn't be able to do this back home. It's just a different situation, but it's more motivation to educate ourselves."

She smiled and hugged me. We would sometimes talk about our life in Colombia, but we all knew that life was gone. Being together brought laughter into our lives. Elizabeth got involved in high school activities, Cynthia got involved in girl scouts, and Louisiana began to feel like home. When Elizabeth turned fifteen, we went to a resale store to buy her a long dress.

"Monita, we need to buy you a quinceañera dress and take pictures. You're the last one to have one, and Cynthia didn't want a celebration. Let's do something special!"

It was a few days before her birthday, and I wanted to have some fun.

"You can all put on makeup and take pictures, but I want to celebrate with pizza, sodas, ice cream, and candles," Cynthia added as we searched the racks for something fancy.

"It's not really a quinceañera, but as long as I don't have to go anywhere with the dress on, it would be fun to get dolled up and pretend," Elizabeth agreed happily.

We found and bought a long beige dress that had been used for a beauty pageant. I fixed Elizabeth's hair, and she applied her own makeup. She felt beautiful that day. We celebrated with balloons and a candlelit dinner, just the four of us; Mom had even requested the evening off. We waltzed to the Blue Danube and pretended we were in a ballroom. While it wasn't a Colombian-style quinceañera, it was filled with love.

THE WEDDING DRESS

All my life, I'd dreamed of being married. I never stopped believing in fairy tales. When I was twenty, I saw an ad in the newspaper for a big wedding dress sale. I went to the store, tried on dresses, and bought one for fifty dollars. When I got home, I ran up the stairway to our apartment, opened the door in a hurry, and excitedly called to my sisters, who were still in high school, to come see the surprise.

"Monita, Cynthia, come down to the living room. You're not going to believe what I bought today."

As they ran down the beige-carpeted stairway, I looked around at the light-salmon walls and took pride in knowing that we had given this room a cozy atmosphere when we had repainted it. I turned the fan on high to cool the room faster, and I can still remember how loud the humming noise got when it was on high.

Suddenly, they were both in front of me, anxiously waiting for me to show them what was in my big white bag.

"I have a wedding dress! I'm getting married!" I giggled and danced around the carpeted living room in between the beige sofas.

"Pamelita, you don't even have a boyfriend!" they responded together, laughing and grabbing the dress bag.

"I want to see it," Cynthia said in disbelief. "It's a real wedding dress. Oh, it's so pretty. But who are you going to marry?"

"It doesn't matter. It means someday, I'm getting married. We need to make this dress beautiful; it needs pearls all over it. I went to Hancock Fabrics and bought several boxes of white pearls. It's called an A-line dress, fitted at the waist and then it flows out. It's a little plain; it needs to be magnificent for my wedding day," I said emphatically.

"I don't like sewing. Can I do something else?" Cynthia asked, looking at me.

"No, we all have to sew pearls. It will be faster that way. Please?" I begged.

"Okay, I will," Cynthia said. "But I don't like doing this, Pamelita. It's stupid."

"Cynthia, this will be fun," Elizabeth said excitedly. "Then we can all use the dress."

That night, we were all sitting around the TV sewing beads when my mother walked in after her three-to-eleven shift at the hospital. Her face depicted her exhaustion.

"How was your night, Mom? I have something to show you." I looked up at her from where I sat on the rug, the dress spread out before me.

"Is that a wedding dress? Who's getting married?" my mom asked slowly as she put down her purse and reached for the white material.

I smiled. "I bought it today, Mom. We're going to fix it up."

"You bought a wedding dress? Why?" she asked.

"I'm getting married, Mom," I said emphatically. "Well, someday I hope to get married." I waited for her approval.

Silence followed for a few minutes while she stared at the dress. Then she sighed. "I'm really tired. I'm going to bed, but we can talk about this later. Be careful with the needle; the netting is very delicate. If you snag the material, you won't be able to fix it."

She was an excellent seamstress and knew her fabrics, so I appreciated her comment. Especially since weddings were the last thing on her mind.

That's when the project truly began. My sisters and I sewed pearls on the dress every evening, and then we would hang it up and admire it.

"It's getting heavier," I said one evening. "We have to be careful with the chiffon; it's lighter and will tear more easily. We can add more pearls on the bodice where the lace is. I like the white flowers it has."

"I think we need to add more to the body," Elizabeth said after I tried it on that day. "This is fun, but I hate when I prick my fingers."

A month and a half later, we looked at it and smiled.

"I believe it's ready. What do you all think?" I asked, admiring the dress.

"It's so beautiful and fluffy," Cynthia said, touching the material.

Elizabeth ran to turn on some music: Johann Pachelbel's Canon in D Major.

"Run, get in line," I called out. "You're the bridesmaids, so you have to walk in front of me."

Elizabeth started walking around the living room, and then Cynthia. Then I followed, wearing my beautiful white dress.

When the music stopped, Elizabeth screamed, "It's my turn now. I want to get married too."

I carefully took off the dress and helped her put it on. We were careful not to tear it as we repeated the procession with Mendelssohn's "Wedding March." Sewing together had created a bond between the three of us. I had never had a boyfriend and had never been kissed, but I knew I was going to have a wedding. Our time with the dress reflected this desire.

By the end of my junior year at LSU, I realized I would need to graduate faster to help my sisters through college. I switched to nursing school at Southeastern Louisiana University. The nursing school was in Baton Rouge, which facilitated transport-tation for me. I continued to work and apply for student loans and grants. Regularly, I checked the school bulletin board for scholarships, which I would apply for. One semester, I received the March of Dimes scholarship, which paid for the rest of my tuition.

In May 1986, I graduated from nursing school, quit all my part-time jobs, and moved to Houston. There, I took a job at Texas Children's Hospital in the pediatric–intermediate unit, a step down from ICU. I worked there for one year and then transferred to their intensive care unit.

In 1987, my brother Juan was accepted to graduate school at LSU in New Orleans, and he finally moved to the States. In New Orleans, he met Elsa, a graduate student in pediatric dentistry. They married in December 1988, and during the summer of 1989, they moved to Houston, where he would complete a fellowship at MD Anderson.

COURTSHIP

In 1988, I was twenty-four years old and working nights. The night I met Fernando, I was taking care of a fourteen-year-old with cystic fibrosis. The patient had gone into renal failure and was intubated, sedated, and on dialysis. I was continually monitoring his vitals due to his delicate status.

"Hello," a doctor said to me as he entered the patient's room. "I'm Dr. Lombana, the nephrology fellow on call tonight. I'll be staying in the room to monitor the patient during his dialysis. He's my sickest patient right now."

He spoke confidently with a strong Spanish accent as he pushed his glasses up his nose with his second finger. I glanced quickly at him, noticing broad shoulders and a small belly. He held the patient's chart on a clipboard in one hand and pulled a chair close to the dialysis machine so he could record the data.

I smiled. "I'm Pamela, his nurse tonight. I don't think I've met you before. He's critical, and his family wants everything possible done for him. I took care of him before he was intobated; he's a nice kid. I'll be at his bedside monitoring him continually, but it's good you're here.

"Where are you from, though?" I asked curiously as I drew blood from the patient for lab work. "You have an accent."

"I'm from Bogotá, Colombia. I went to medical school there, but I did my pediatric residency at Driscoll in Corpus Christi." He looked up from the patient's chart and smiled. "I've been in

25

Houston for a year now, and I love the city. Are you *Paisa*?" He chuckled.

"I'm from Medellín, but I've been in the States for seven years now. I thought you might be Colombian. I haven't met many in Houston, though I just moved here a year and half ago." As I spoke, I alternated between suctioning, procedures and charting, and trying to steal a glance or two at the doctor, all while keeping my eyes on the heart and vital signs monitors.

He laughed. "What are we doing speaking in English, then?" He began chatting with me in Spanish, and we spent the rest of night talking as we worked.

Once the dialysis was finished, he picked up the patient's chart to leave. He stopped at the doorway and turned around. "I'm going to get some food from the McDonald's on the first floor. Can I get you something?"

"I'll take a tea to help me stay awake," I said, admiring how thoughtful it was of him to ask.

He came back with the tea and a warm chocolate chip cookie.

"They just took them out of the oven, so I couldn't resist and got two. One for you and one for me. I'd like to talk to you more, but I have to leave now. Could I call you this week?" He was smiling expectantly.

"Yes, I'll give you my number. I work tomorrow, but then I'm off for a couple of days." I tried not to sound too excited as I wrote my phone number down on a piece of paper.

Fernando had spent five hours in the room with me beside the patient, and my shift was almost over. The patient survived the night, though he died a week later. His family was devastated. All the nurses who had taken care of him cried with the family. The pain of the parents who lost the child pierced the heart of everyone in the ICU. The family had wanted everything possible done in hopes that he would recover, but it didn't happen.

The following week, I received a call. My heart leaped with excitement.

"Pamela, do you remember me? Fernando Lombana? I'm off tomorrow night. Would you like to go to dinner with me?"

I had recognized his voice as soon as I picked up the phone. I was glad he had called, and I didn't hesitate to answer.

"Yes, I would love to," I responded. "I don't have anything going on."

"How about Houston's? Have you been to that restaurant?"

"Houston's? I don't think I've been there. Do you want me to meet you there, or will you pick me up?" I was smiled excitedly. I hadn't had a date in a long time.

"I'll pick you up. Can you be ready by seven?" There was an enthusiasm in his voice that made me feel happy.

"Yes, I'll be off, so I can be ready. Let me give you my address." I proceeded to tell him how to get to my apartment complex.

The conversation with Fernando during dinner flowed easily, as we had a wide range of topics to discuss. It didn't even matter to me that he was on call and his beeper kept ringing. This was before cell phones, so each time, he would go to the hostess and ask to use the restaurant's phone. I might have eaten most of my dinner alone, but I enjoyed myself. I understood the demands he dealt with as a nephrology fellow. What mattered was that I was on a date and it felt right.

That was the beginning of our whirlwind relationship.

Our first date was cut short because he was paged to return to the hospital. It was a transplant patient who was in critical condition. He drove me home. Before he left, he asked, "Can I take you out again? It's been pretty hectic tonight."

"Yes, of course." I walked into my apartment smiling. He wanted to see me again. I couldn't wait to tell my friends.

The next week, he dropped by to say hi when I was working the night shift and invited me out again. "I'm going to dinner with my sister and her boyfriend this Saturday. He's French, so we're going to La Colombe d'Or. I'd like you to meet her. Are you off?"

"Yes, I can go. I'll switch shifts with someone. I've never been there," I answered, feeling special. "Is your sister going to be okay meeting me on your second date?"

He broke out in laughter. "Of course, she's my sister."

That evening, I found out he spoke French fluently. He had gone to the French school in Colombia. I was impressed with his command of the language. I had taken French in college and finished with a C.

One day when I was off, my sister Elizabeth and I decided to go to Galveston for the day. When Fernando found out we were going to the beach, he took the day off to go with us. Elizabeth and I were delighted to have company. The three of us spent the day at the beach, playing, talking, and laughing. He loved being surrounded by people and loved being in the spotlight. He told us jokes, making us laugh all day. As Elizabeth and I returned to Houston, we discussed how lucky I was to have found such a nice person.

One weekend, Fernando invited me to go to Corpus Christi, where he had done his pediatric residency. He was co-owner of a photo development shop, along with another doctor and that doctor's nephew. He told me about the business and how his ideas had helped with marketing the company. He had asked me to bring dressy clothes for a special occasion, and I'd been thrilled, believing it would be a romantic date at a restaurant on the beach. When we arrived at the photo shop, however, he had a special request.

"Juan, this is my girlfriend, Pamela. We'd like to get some portraits taken of us together. We've been dating for a few months, and I want one for my study." Fernando smiled at me, holding my hand. I was touched by this. I knew it meant I was special to him.

Dating someone who was in residency or fellowship meant taking advantage of every little opportunity to see them because there could be days or weeks of not seeing them. So I was always looking for ways to have contact with him.

We talked on the phone and saw each other whenever we could, but we didn't really spend a lot of time together due to hectic schedules. I still worked nights, and he was a fellow who moonlighted at the emergency room on the weekends. I loved to go visit him in the ER and take him food.

We dated for several months and got engaged in December.

I had met someone from the country in which I grew up. We shared the same language, the same faith, and love of the same food. We laughed at each other's native jokes, and we were both in health fields.

Being able to talk in Spanish and laugh at jokes in Spanish took the homesickness away. The emptiness I had felt when I first came to the States was replaced by a sense of connection. I didn't feel like a foreigner in a distant land anymore. I belonged, but now I had two worlds. My American world, which was work and my nursing friends, and my Spanish world with Fernando. Little by little, other Hispanic friends became our family.

Fernando loved knowledge, reading, and learning. He was funny, witty and had a good sense of humor. At twenty-four, I was fascinated and captivated by him, and I fell madly in love. It was a dream come true.

ALCOHOL

Alcohol comes into your life slowly. When you are young, he knocks at the door politely. Once you let him in and he feels comfortable, he wants to stay. He brings laughter and tears, you think he brings courage, but in reality, he brings chaos, unless you can stop him. He can become the unwanted guest in your house. He will take over your home, your family, and your life if you are not aware of his silent presence.

Alcohol sometimes travels with laughter, but most of the time for us, he came with fear. The fear had always been sleeping, but it started waking up after I was wed.

Alcohol was always the third companion on our dates. He was called whiskey, and he liked being on the rocks. I didn't grow up around him, so I was unaware of the power he had. He was our invisible companion. We often double-dated with my best friend at the time, and the evenings always ended in some type of disagreement. But Alcohol never took responsibility and was quick to blame others.

"He drinks too much," Fernando would say. "He really loses his temper. Your coworker's husband is crazy." I believed him. I believed it was all the fault of my coworker's husband.

"Yes, he does seem to drink a lot," I would agree. Whiskey was never guilty. He quietly sat in the background until the next date, where he was present, participating, and opening Pandora's box, allowing feelings of anger, paranoia, and mistrust to emerge.

One evening, my coworker Mary and her husband, Tony, went to Houston's with us on a double date. The lights were dim, the food was delicious and affordable for young couples, and there was energy in the restaurant. When the waiter came around to take orders for drinks, the men started with scotch on the rocks. Mary and I were happy to be on a date, and we each ordered a screwdriver.

"Hey, Tony," Fernando said laughingly. "I bet I know more about the American Revolution than you do. Ask me a question, anything. I could probably beat you at trivia."

I smiled at him. He was good at trivia, and I knew he could win on almost any subject. I was proud to be with him and loved the challenge, especially if we were on the same team.

"American History? You are crazy. I grew up here; you didn't," Tony said, accepting the challenge.

They began quizzing each other, continuing the game throughout dinner. The drinks flowed. At first, we were all laughing and participating, enjoying the questions. As the evening progressed, their tones of voice changed, and anger replaced the playfulness of the moment. Mary and I looked at each other nervously. I glanced at my watch and noticed it was getting late.

"Fernando, I worked last night. I'm really tired, and I want to go home," I said, trying to de-escalate the situation.

"This asshole thinks he knows more about history than I do," Fernando said aggressively, looking at Tony. "What's his problem?"

"I really want to go now," I replied. "It's just a game." I looked at Mary, who was also trying to diffuse the tension.

"Yes, the babysitter is waiting for us. We need to go. And I think I should drive," she told Tony.

"Are you saying I have a problem?" Tony asked, sounding agitated. "Because I don't." He pulled the keys from her hands.

"No, I just want to go home," she replied quietly.

Fernando turned and handed me the keys. "You drive. I can't take the chance with my license." On the way home, he started venting.

"Could you believe him, challenging me on my knowledge?" His tone was aggressive and his eyes on me. "I may not have grown up here, but I know more than he does. I'll always be smarter, and I don't like being challenged or questioned by ignorant people."

I listened quietly, keeping my eyes on the road. I didn't want to contradict him, but I knew it wasn't a one-way street. They had both lost control and been rude and angry.

The next day, I talked to Mary and tried to understand what we could do to avoid the situation from escalating next time. Everything we tried was useless. Once the third glass of scotch on the rocks was consumed, the tension began. The altercations continued until we decided it wasn't worth it to go on double dates. She and I remained friends for many years, but we both avoided having our husbands interact. In the years to come, this pattern would repeat, eventually leading to our social isolation.

MARRIAGE

In May 1989, at the age of twenty-five, I walked down the aisle. I didn't wear the wedding dress I had bought several years before because I couldn't find it. I had moved several times, and eventually, it was misplaced or left behind. So I borrowed from a friend a white princess-style floor-length dress with long sleeves. It didn't look like my original dress. It was prettier and had a longer train.

I felt beautiful.

Fernando was on his last year of residency, and I was working nights. In the first few months, I realized marriage wasn't a fairy tale. During that first year, he lost his temper frequently.

We bought a house right after our wedding, which put a financial burden on both of us. Since we were both working, I had assumed we would share the chores. However, it soon became clear that housekeeping and cooking were not our jobs, but mine.

We were both from traditional backgrounds, in which the man was the main provider and the woman took care of the house and children. I believed it was normal for me to take on that role, and I couldn't understand why I felt exhausted all the time.

It was also common for him to check the kitchen drawers or the closets. He frequently went into a rage, pulling the drawers out and throwing everything on the floor, if he felt they weren't organized correctly.

After three years, I hired someone to come weekly to help with the cleaning, yet even that wasn't enough. Eventually, I would hire a full-time housekeeper to try to avoid his angry outbursts. It was money well spent to help relieve the stress.

One evening, three months after our wedding day, I sat down to balance our checkbook in the breakfast room. It was off by five dollars. I went to look for him in the study to see if he could find the discrepancy.

The study was the only room we had been able to have custom built. It had dark-stained wooden bookshelves along the back wall and a dark wooden desk with two chairs: a reading chair and a black leather chair. The floor was covered in beige carpet, and the windows were draped with light green-gray curtains.

"Fernando, the checkbook isn't balancing. Could you please help me find the mistake?"

He was sitting behind the desk, working on the computer. When I approached him, he looked up and stared at me. I watched him realize what I had said. His face changed as he pushed his chair back and stood. He started hitting the desk as his voice escalated.

"What do you mean, it doesn't balance? Are you stupid? Don't you know how to do that? It has always balanced for me, down to the last penny. I want to see the statement."

He was silent for a moment, and I was too stunned to speak. We just stared at each other.

"I said, I want to see the statements. This one and last month's."

I was frozen. No one had ever screamed at me that way my entire life. He grabbed a book that sat on the desk and threw it across the room. The bang as it hit the paneling made me jump. He paced the room as I remained still with the statements in my hands, unable to move due to shock. Fernando approached me and tore the statements from my hands.

"I can't find the discrepancy. I don't know where it is. It's not a mistake made on purpose," I answered quietly, taken aback by his reaction. I didn't want to upset him more.

Fear had entered the room.

"So are you saying I didn't record every check I wrote in the checkbook? I always record everything," he screamed. "I always do it correctly. If it doesn't balance for you, maybe you need to take some accounting classes and learn." He threw the statements on the floor.

I left the room as fast as I could and ran outside. I needed air. I felt exhausted. My head was spinning. I sat on the curb, shaking and sobbing. *What did I do? Who is he? Who did I marry?* I asked myself as I continued to cry. Time went by — maybe five minutes, maybe an hour — and I heard him come outside. He sat beside me and held me close.

"I'm sorry. I'm really sorry. Please don't cry. It won't happen again. It always balanced before. I just got upset, but it doesn't mean anything. You know I love you. I won't ever scream again. Forgive me," he said in a soothing voice.

After a moment of silence, I answered, having believed his apology. "Yes, I'll forgive you. I love you too."

The next day, I received flowers and a beautiful card telling me how much he loved me. He also posted sticky notes with love messages on our bathroom mirror all week long. That week, I received my first piece of jewelry from Tiffany: a pair of delicate sapphire earrings. I held them in my hands and thanked him. I still believed I had a good marriage and that nothing could go wrong.

This behavior, however, would become a habit and would intensify over time. Outbursts followed by words of regret. Outbursts followed by flowers. Outbursts followed by jewelry.

Two months after the checkbook incident, Fernando came home with a brochure for a medical nephrology conference in Washington, DC.

"Pamelita, make sure you're off for five days in November, between the fifteenth and the twenty-first. I'm going to this conference, and I'm taking you with me. You can tour the museums while I attend the conference, and in the evenings, we'll do things together. You'll need to buy winter clothes because it'll be cold."

"Wow, that's great. I've never been to Washington. I'll request the time off tomorrow. I'm so happy we're going together." I embraced him lovingly. *Life is wonderful,* I thought. *I love being married.*

A few weeks after our return from Washington, we were both at home after working seven straight twelve-hours shifts. He was telling me about helping a homeless man he had seen on the streets.

"Pamelita, do you remember the man who stands on the corner of Williams Trace and Lexington?"

"Yes, the older man. The one we give food to sometimes?" I looked at him curiously.

"That one. Well, I went to the Kmart close to there and bought him a thick jacket for the winter and some food. It's colder, and he doesn't have enough clothes. He was so happy when he received it, he kept thanking me. I need to help the poor. That's what really makes me happy."

He was smiling. I felt a deep connection to his words, and I understood what he meant. That evening, we stayed home and watched movies while eating Domino's pizza. I was proud to be his wife.

The next day, his mood changed drastically.

"Pamelita, come here. Come see what I'm looking at." His voice was raised forcefully, almost to a screaming pitch. "Do you see what I see?" He pointed to a sock in the corner of his closet.

"It's one of your socks," I said, stunned by his reaction. "What's wrong with it?"

"I've left it there for a week to see when you would notice it and pick it up." His face was red as a beet.

"Fernando, it's your sock and your closet."

"It's my house, and I pay most of the bills because I make more money. This is your job." He picked up the sock and threw it in the washing bin. Before I could reply, he walked off. I stood in the closet and took deep breaths before leaving the room.

In April 1991, my oldest daughter, Christina, was born. My brother, Juan, and my sister-in-law, Elsa, had spent the night with me in the hospital while I was in labor. Fernando had slept through the night on the hospital couch; he had worked the night before and not slept during the day. We were both ecstatic with the arrival of our new daughter. She brought joy into our lives.

The day we left the hospital with the baby, Fernando had a surprise for me.

"Pamelita, you are now the queen and the baby is the princess, so I got us a limousine for our drive home." He beamed.

"Fercito, that is so sweet of you." I felt honored and loved as I found my seat beside the baby in the spacious car.

In beautiful moments like that, it was easy just to love him. Nothing else mattered.

REUNITED WITH DAD
1992

One evening in December 1991, Elizabeth came to the house after work. I could see she was eager to tell me something, but she wanted to sit down in the living room first.

The living room was decorated with lights and smelled of fresh pine. The Christmas tree was six feet tall, and we had decorated it the week before with an assortment of Christmas balls. The beauty and excitement of the holiday was portrayed all around the house. Christina was ten months old, and I had just found out I was pregnant again. The lights on the Christmas tree reminded me that Christmas was always a season of hope and family.

"Pamelita, I have great news," Elizabeth said once we were seated on the sofa. "My boss wants me to go to Colombia and help translate the meeting with Ecopetrol. They are going to pay for everything. We leave in January and will be gone for a week. This is an opportunity for me to find Papi."

I was stunned, and I stared at her in disbelief.

"Monita, that's not going to be easy. Nobody knows where he is, but if you're there, it will be easier than searching from here. What an opportunity! If you find him, you need to tell him he has grandkids. I'm so happy for you." We hugged each other.

When we pulled back from the embrace, I asked, "How are you going to find him?"

"I don't know, but someone has to know something about him. It's been almost ten years since we heard anything about him."

"I know; I miss him. He doesn't even know I'm married or that I have a daughter."

"Life has been hard for us," Elizabeth said. "We moved, then there was the divorce and not being able to go back to Colombia, and then losing dad. It makes me really sad. I was thirteen the last time I saw him. I don't want to find out someday that he died without us ever seeing him again. I miss him."

"Talk to all of our aunts; it's a big family. I hope you find him. We'll tell Juan and Cynthia if you do."

There was a tinge of pain in my heart as I remembered how I missed him and how it seemed like he had disappeared from the earth.

Elizabeth's business trip was short, but I anxiously awaited her return, hoping she found some answers. Her flight back from Colombia arrived in Houston's international airport around one in the afternoon, and I took Christina with me when I went to pick her up. When Elizabeth exited the glass doors from the international flights and saw Christina, she ran over and picked her up.

"Mimi, Mimi." Christina clapped her hands as she excitedly repeated her nickname for Elizabeth. Elizabeth swung her through the air as they both laughed. Then Elizabeth turned to me.

"Pamelita, he's alive!" she exclaimed happily. "He's in California. No one in Colombia had heard from him, so the aunts started calling around to all the family members. One distant cousin of theirs knew he had moved to the States with his new wife. All they knew was that he's in Los Angeles, but it can't be hard to find him now that we know the city."

I hugged her, tears of relief streaming down my cheeks.

When I went home, I ran to find Fernando. "I have great news! My dad is alive and in the States. Elizabeth tracked him to Los Angeles."

Fernando was sitting at his desk when I entered. He stood and came over to me, a big smile on his face.

"That is wonderful news. We'll find your dad, just like we found my mother's family in Mexico. The best thing is, he's alive and not dead like my mother's mom was." He hugged me for a moment. "Los Angeles is pretty big, but all we need is a phone book. I'll order it now."

As he went to figure out how he could order one, I laughed. "This is amazing. We are both finding our lost families. It must be Christinas' birth."

Fernando ordered a Los Angeles phone book, which arrived the next week. When it arrived, Elizabeth and I felt like we had discovered a box full of treasures, and we flipped through the pages containing all the telephone numbers of the residents of Los Angeles.

We searched for Mario Echeverri. To our surprise, there were three pages of Marios with the same last name. Elizabeth and I looked at each other with determination. We were on a quest.

The next weeks were filled with numerous phone calls as we went down the list in the phone book. We made a lot of phone calls and tried not to get discouraged. This went on for days, until Elizabeth finally called the right number.

"This is Mario Echeverri's residence. Can I help you?" It was a deep voice with a strong *Paisa* accent.

"Papi?" Her voice shook.

"Who is this?"

"Papi, it's your daughter, Monita. I've missed you."

She started crying, emotions of a lifetime coming together. His voice trembled. Soft muffled crying could be heard in his voice as he struggled to speak over the phone.

"My children have found me. My children have found me." He broke down crying before he could continue the conversation.

She called us all, and one by one, we all dialed him. We were so excited to reconnect with dad. Finally, I picked up the phone.

He answered, and I could tell he had been waiting for the call.

"Papi, how are you? It's been ten years since I last saw you, and I've really missed you," I cried. "I'm so happy Monita found you."

"Pamelita, it has been my prayer to see you all again. I am so sorry for the way things happened." There was a tinge of regret in his voice.

"Papi, I love you. I can't believe we will be able to see you soon. You have grandkids, and they will get to know you now."

"I'm sorry I didn't walk you down the aisle and that I missed the birth of your daughter. I wish I could go back in time and be there for you."

"Papi, now you will. When can you come visit us? It's cheaper for you to come to Houston than for the whole family to go to LA."

"I can come any weekend. Can I bring my wife to meet you?"

Silence stretched as I considered my feelings about that. *No, no, it's our time,* I thought.

"Papi, why don't you come alone this first time. Give us time to be with you and catch up."

"I understand. Another time," he said reassuringly.

My siblings and I planned a weekend with my father in Lake Conroe. Mom had asked to join us so she could see him, but my father refused to have her there. The refusal didn't dampen our enthusiasm, though. Elsa and I were both five-months pregnant and so excited that our children would have another grandfather.

The entire family was filled with anticipation when Juan and Elsa went to pick our father up from the airport. When they arrived at my house, my sisters and I ran to him and hugged him. Tears flowed down our cheeks as years of pain that had been bottled up slowly released. Tears that soothed the soul. The tears were soon followed by laughter. Hearing his voice after so many years was comforting. My father was a big story-teller. He started telling us about his journey to Los Angeles and the different jobs he had performed. The life of the immigrant who works in all types of jobs to feed his family. As we learned of his struggles, we wished we could have been there to support him. Our hearts were filled with compassion.

That weekend, we all went to Lake Conroe, where Fernando and I owned a two-bedroom townhome a couple of blocks from the lake. It had white walls and tiled flooring that ranged in tone from beige to pink. The first floor was a small kitchen and rectangular room that could have been used for a dining and living room. There was a large sliding glass door that looked onto a wide green grassy area in the back. It was cozy.

All nine of us slept there, and we spent the weekend fishing, boating, talking, laughing, and playing dominoes. The love of the weekend brought forgiveness and healing. We let go of un-resolved pain. We were delighted to have our father back in our lives. Time had stopped. Ten years of silence had been broken.

During our last evening together, stories from our childhood were retold over and over in between laughter and tears of joy.

"Mario," Fernando said at one point. "Pamelita has always said that you were a great fisherman. I can't wait for you to teach me some of your secrets."

"Fernando," my dad said, smiling at him. "You have a lake and a boat. What else do you need to fish? If there is water, there are fish."

They laughed together. It felt good to see their connection. That moment filled me with joy.

On the last evening, my father said, "I had prayed and asked God not let me die without seeing my children." His voice was filled with gratitude as he looked at all of us.

"Papi, we are together now," I said happily. "We have to plan how we'll continue seeing each other." I was already dreaming of those future reunions.

"There hasn't been a day that I haven't thought about you. Not a single day. I've missed you all." He said this as he held his two granddaughters in his lap: Valentina, my brothers' only child at the time, and Christina. "It's going to be hard to say goodbye at the airport," he added, tears streaming down his cheeks.

You left us. We were children then. We would never leave you. These silent thoughts crossed my mind in those moments. Motherhood had awakened feelings of love stronger than I had ever known possible for a human being. I thought about my daughter and the baby to be born, and I couldn't imagine a life without them. *Why didn't you look for us?* I wondered before rapidly dismissing the thought. I was not going to dwell on the past. We had him now.

"I'm going to have benign prostate surgery in two weeks," he told us. "It's a pretty simple procedure, but I'll be in the hospital for a few days. Then I want to move to Houston. I want to be close to my children."

"Yes, we want you close. We have missed you, and you need to be part of the expanding family." I indicated my sister-in-law's belly and my own. "They'll be born the same day. Isn't that amazing?"

That weekend was a gift. Two weeks later, my father went into the hospital for prostate surgery. On the third day after the surgery, he called all of us to tell us how well he was doing. His last conversation was with my brother, Juan. He told him he loved him and how happy he was to have found his kids. After they hung up, Juan resumed his work. Ten minutes later, my father stood up to use the restroom and collapsed. He died instantly from a bilateral pulmonary embolism. The hospital called Juan to give him the news, telling him it was an instant death. After composing himself, he called me.

"Pamelita, it's Juan," he said, crying. "Papi just died. I'm coming over."

I sat on a chair in the breakfast room, put my face in my hands, and cried. No words can express the grief I felt when I received the news of his death. There was only deep pain.

After a while, I called Cynthia and Elizabeth. Cynthia was living in Louisiana, so I spoke with her first. Then I called Elizabeth and told her to come to my house. I couldn't tell her the news over the phone. When she arrived, my brother was already there. We all stood around the kitchen table.

"Elizabeth," I said as I approached her. "We have something to tell you. We didn't want to tell you over the phone."

"What is it? What happened? It's something with Papi, isn't it?" She gave a nervous laugh that broke into tears. "What happened? Tell me what's wrong."

I held her in my arms as I broke the news. "Dad is dead. He died two hours ago." She started screaming and pulled away.

"No, no, no. He can't be dead! We just found him." She crumpled to the kitchen floor, crying. I knelt and held her tightly until the uncontrollable sobbing quietly stopped.

Juan reminded us that Papi's last words had been about how happy he was to have found us again. His prayers had been answered, and so had ours. We were able to see him before his death.

We all flew to Los Angeles for his funeral. Fernando paid for all the airfare, and I was moved by his generosity at that moment. When we arrived, my father's wife met us at the airport. She took us to their home, a one-bedroom apartment with scarce furniture. Looking around the complex and inside his apartment, I knew his financial situation had been difficult. In his bedroom, all our baby pictures had been glued to the wall. In his wallet was a small faded prayer card for St. Jude, the patron saint of desperate cases and lost causes. It was apparently a prayer he said daily until his last breath.

For the next year, there was pain mixed with emotions of gratitude in our hearts. Our lives went back to the way they were before we had found and reunited with our father. The emptiness, however, had gone away. Even though he had died, we were finally at peace. We had had a chance to forgive, to say "I'm sorry," "Thank you," and "I love you," and to see our father before he died.

His death also brought healing to our mother. She had always loved him and going from divorced to widowed brought closure to her life with him.

In July, my niece Andrea was born. Two weeks later, in August, my son, Nicholas, was born — one day after my fathers' birthday.

THE SEED

When I met Fernando, he was the life of the party. He could talk about any subject, carry on any conversation, make any joke, and argue any case. Everything he did was done with intensity. I saw him as hardworking, brilliant, and dedicated to helping the poor.

One evening, when we were out for dinner at Pappasito's Cantina eating fajitas, he started telling me stories of his last year in Colombia.

"I want to help the poor. The rich have enough doctors," he said, making me feel proud and connected to him. "My happiest time in medical school was my last year of service in the countryside—'*mi año rural.*' I was in a village in Colombia close to Villavicencio. Poverty, hunger, and guerilla warfare had struck this town, but I was able to make a difference there. I was *El Doctorcito.* I was somebody." He was smiling.

In my head, I could visualize the humble hospital he described, with two small rooms, a single examination table, and a dirt floor. The operating room had a wooden table, a head lamp, and a small table that held the few surgical supplies, along with a copy of the textbook *Gray's Anatomy* for reference. I imagined Fernando surrounded by people needing his help.

"I performed a hysterectomy on the prostitute of the village because she was bleeding continually. She paid me back with a puppy I named Syphilis. The dog followed me everywhere

46

I went. She became my companion, but when I left Colombia to come to the States, Syphilis refused to eat and starved to death."

"You named her Syphilis?" I asked in disbelief, laughing out loud.

"Yes, and she was the best dog I ever had. I hated to leave her, but I didn't have a choice." He then moved on to other stories, and I listened to them all in awe.

I loved hearing about the people he had helped and the surgeries he had performed with *Gray's Anatomy* open beside him. He could be such a charmer. Slowly, I started idolizing him. He seemed to have it all together.

We carried on intellectual conversations, but we couldn't discuss any feelings. Emotions were a sign of weakness to Fernando. Since I came from a broken home, his family looked picture perfect from the outside. But family secrets slowly emerged in those first years of marriage.

The seeds of abuse had been planted in his heart during his childhood. The unresolved pain and anger of the unprotected child would surface throughout our marriage. He had been the victim of physical and verbal abuse growing up. The perpetrator of the abuse had been his mother, Teresa.

One evening, while we were listening to the news, a story came on about a child who had been abused. Turning to me, Fernando said, "When I was in my third year of medical school, I had a fight with my older brother. My mother became angry and took his side. She started screaming and slapped me in the face. I reacted immediately, grabbing her by the neck and lifting her off the floor. I pushed her against the wall and told her, 'If you ever touch me again, I will kill you. Hear me? I will kill you.' It was the last time in her life that she laid a hand on me."

He spoke the words with a strong voice, full of conviction and full of anger. His expression had tightened as his face blushed.

I listened in quiet amazement, thinking to myself, *She must have really hit him a lot to create such a strong reaction. She deserved it.* But it was a red flag that I didn't see. Behaviors learned, behaviors repeated, behaviors that creep slowly into peoples lives—they are hard to see in the moment. As I continued to learn more about his childhood, I realized he needed help to deal with his past.

One day after work as we sat at the dinner table, I broached the subject. "Fernando, I've been thinking it might be a good idea for you to talk with a psychologist about your past."

"Are you fucking crazy?" he demanded, looking at me angrily. "Are you suggesting I'm crazy? That's mental masturbation. I don't need that. I'm smarter than all of them. What can they tell me that I don't know?" As he continued, his voice rose to a scream. "I don't wash my dirty laundry in public. This conversation is over."

He stood up, slammed the table, and stomped out of the room. I was left cold. I avoided him for a while that evening so he could cool down. He later came over to me, laughing and joking.

"Sorry I screamed. I'm just really stressed at work. Let's go to the lake this weekend and forget about this. Let's invite Juan and Elsa."

"I'd love to go to the lake," I replied, happy to change subjects. "Sounds like a plan." The next day, I received orchids, one of my favorite flowers. It would be years before I suggested any psychological help again.

We arrived at Lake Conroe on Friday evening and woke up Saturday morning to go water-skiing. Juan had been teaching us how to ski, so we were all excited to practice. Elsa and I went first and had no problem enjoying ourselves as long as we stayed behind the boat. We were still learning how to cross from side to side.

Then it was Fernando and Juan's turn.

I drove the boat while Juan gave Fernando instructions. He was having trouble standing on the skis, and he started screaming, "Switch drivers, Pamela. You keep drowning me."

My brother immediately took over at the wheel, whispering to me, "It's not your fault. He's not in shape."

After a few more tries with Juan driving, he still couldn't manage to get up. At last, he called for a stop, and we pulled him into the boat. No one said anything. We all understood his frustration.

Finally, he turned to me, angry. "What the fuck were you doing? Why can you drive correctly for other people, but not me?" I knew I was a good driver, but me pulling him was always an opportunity for him to scream at me. Eventually, I completely avoided driving if he was trying to ski. Someone else could take his screaming. I didn't want to deal with it.

Fernando had stories of love and hate. Stories that were as precious to him as secrets, unshared until we had been married for a couple of years. He loved his father, Alberto, the pilot. Alberto had had two parallel families, so his time had been divided and scarce for each. The first family had known nothing of the second, but the second family was always aware of the first. Two separate families, two women in love with the same man—eventually, it all came to light.

When the youngest daughter of the first family was fifteen years old, they found out he had a second family. In a family confrontation, that youngest daughter asked Alberto to leave. She had the courage her mother didn't. He'd kept all of it a secret for eighteen years in a country where divorce was not recognized and the children of unwed mothers were called bastards and sometimes refused baptism.

Fernando had been the third child of the second family.

Whenever Alberto came home to Fernando's family, his Cessna aircraft would be filled with presents, and the house would be filled with laughter. The abuse doled out by Fernando's mother would cease, though it quickly resumed when his father left. Fernando both loved and hated his mother. He loved her intelligence and her brilliance as a painter and a violinist, but he couldn't stand the woman who always had to be smarter than everyone around her. The woman who always created conflict between him and his brothers. Eventually, it separated them forever.

Fernando hated the woman who would beat him until he bled. He shared with me the story of a beating his mother had given him when he was ten. The school bus driver had told her that Fernando had used foul language when he picked him up for school. That evening, she beat Fernando in the face with a shoe until he bled. The next morning, when the bus driver arrived, he cried when he saw Fernando's beaten face, his bruised eyes that were almost completely closed, and his broken, swollen lips. That day, the bus driver became his friend.

Fernando frequently received beatings with a belt, until his body was marked and bruised—punishments that would be considered child abuse today, even in Colombia. He had memories of being forced out of the car, only to be left behind as he watched his mom drive off with his siblings.

It was a story of abandonment.

How does someone learn to love if all they've experienced is a loveless life? How do they know whether the punishment they dole out is too harsh if they themselves survived it as a child? These were behaviors that Fernando engaged in, even though he had promised he never would.

Abuse is a generational cycle that must be broken.

I still remember Fernando's words when our first child, Christina, was born and we were driving home with her in a car seat. "I can't discipline her. I don't ever want to hurt her. I don't ever want her to feel the pain and shame I felt. I still carry anger toward my mother, and I can't forgive her. I was a child." His words hung in the air. I heard them, but I couldn't understand then how they would eventually change our life.

The secrets slowly came out over time, the stories of the past that remained in his mind. Flashbacks haunted him. When I heard these stories, I wanted to protect him from his past. I believed that if he felt loved, he would heal. I didn't understand that his wounds were still bleeding. He needed help, and I couldn't fix it.

TERESA

When Fernando's mother, Teresa, was six years old, she and her sister, Carmina, were kidnapped by their father, Tomás. He took them from their home in Tampico, Mexico, to live in Colombia.

Desperate to find them, their mother, Antonina, went to her father, a Russian immigrant, begging for help and money to find them. However, she had married Tomás against her father's will, which her father reminded her of as he turned his back on her. Without his help, she couldn't leave Mexico. He refused to release her passport, and she lacked funds.

She sent letters to Colombia asking for her daughters to please be returned to her. Letters that were never opened, letters that ended up in the trash. Six months after their arrival in Colombia, Tomás died from sepsis and a kidney infection. Teresa and Carmina were pretty much orphans then. Nobody wanted to take care of them, yet no one thought of returning them to their mother.

Tomás's girlfriend, Maria, decided to raise the two girls. She was a religious fanatic who believed the girls' fate was due to their parents' sins. She attributed Tomás's death to a punishment from heaven. According to her, the girls had to be taught right and were in need of spiritual cleansing.

Teresa and Carmina lived a life of severe physical and verbal abuse, which only ended for each of them when they eloped.

However, the cycle resumed when they married and became mothers. The victims then became the perpetrators of the abuse.

This is the shame that abuse carries for human beings. Children observe and repeat behaviors and roles learned in life. These behaviors can be changed, if acknowledged. Otherwise, they can destroy the ones stuck in the cycle.

1995

When we were dating, Fernando would always have a drink or two, but at twenty-five years old, I didn't know it would eventually take over our lives after we'd married. I believed he was a good person, but under the influence of alcohol, his erratic behavior became exacerbated, and fear came into my life.

When our children, Christina, Nicholas, and Natalia, were born, it was the best time of our life together. Laughter and excitement mixed with tears, but it was a balance. In 1992, Fernando opened a pediatric clinic. I started working with him part-time, helping with the administration and nursing department. Being in the clinic was good for Fernando. He loved to help people, and when he saw a need, he didn't think twice.

If he found out a patient was going to be evicted, he would pay their rent. If a patient couldn't afford medical care, he wouldn't charge them. He loved to carry small water guns in his pockets and tease the pediatric patients by squirting them with water. This would make the kids giggle and duck, and the mothers smile.

He also had great moments with his staff. If it had been a hard week, he would take them out to happy hour. The clinic's Christmas party was always the highlight of the year. The staff and their children were all included. Fernando would dress up as Santa Claus and have a present for all the kids, as well as bonuses for the staff.

But it wasn't always sunshine in the clinic. Fernando's moods were hard to decipher.

One day, Fernando arrived in a bad mood. Everything seemed to set him off. After lunch, he started screaming.

"Stupid women, what do you think you all are doing? Can't you all do anything right? I'm surrounded by fucking idiots. Do I need to do everything around here? Pamela, what morons did you hire? You are all fired; get the hell out of my clinic."

He stomped to his office, slammed the door, and locked himself in. I couldn't stop the staff from leaving. I had to close the clinic at that moment. I sat in stunned silence, not daring to disturb him. I couldn't believe what he had just done. How would we manage the clinic without our staff? I called the *Greensheet* to put out an ad for medical assistants.

Before too long, he came into my office. "I need you to call everyone back. I just had a bad moment; it doesn't mean anything. They all know me. Tell them they have their jobs back with a raise." Then he walked out.

I picked up the phone and called everyone individually, making excuses for his outburst. I begged them to come back. Half the staff returned the next morning. When he arrived, he told them he was sorry and gave each person five hundred dollars and a new VCR.

They were ecstatic. "*Doctorcito*, we love you. We know you get stressed," one of the medical assistants said, holding the gift close to her chest.

One day in 1995, Fernando hired a nurse practitioner from Washington. She sparked in me the desire to become a pediatric nurse practitioner. Natalia was a year old when I went back to school and four when I graduated. I studied in the children's game room because I wasn't allowed to leave my books on the desk in the study.

This came about one evening during my first semester of graduate school, in the summer of 1996. I had a project due. I had been working in our downstairs study, where there was quiet and privacy. The room had floor-to-ceiling bookshelves and a semicircular desk on which the computer sat. Under it, there were multiple shelves for files, which were kept locked. I never gave it much thought, but I had never had access to those. There was a big space on the surface of the desk, where we could place two to three open books at a time if we were working on a research project.

Fernando walked in that evening and said, "You really need to find another place to study. This is my desk and my room. You can study anywhere you want, but not here."

"Fernando, what do you mean? It's our study," I said. I watched him shut all my books and put them in a pile. As the banging of the books filled the room, my body tensed. My heart beat faster as I wondered where this was going.

"No, not our study. Mine. I don't want to find your books on my desk, or I will simply throw them away." He was almost screaming as he stared at me.

"You're kidding, right?" I asked, trying to make a joke but also seeing if I could push the line.

His eyes and his posture told me that he had made his decision and I needed to move out of his space. A wave of exhaustion fell over me. I no longer felt that the situation was worth arguing over. Little by little, I was losing ground, but I never realized it.

"No, I'm not, Pamelita. You can go to graduate school, but you don't study in this room. This is my room."

I picked up my books and left. I went to the children's game room and placed my books on one of their desks. Every fight or discussion took energy, and I was starting to feel tired all the time. I simply adjusted without protesting. I found myself apologizing frequently, saying "I'm sorry" to appease him and settle situations.

Getting this degree was already difficult with children, but I was determined. I told myself that it would be a good example for them to see me studying and it would be easier for me to check their homework and assignments if I was in the same area. If I rationalized, I could bury the feelings of humiliation and worthlessness of being a grown woman who was treated like a child.

When I graduated, Fernando threw a big party with mariachis and catered food. He told everyone how proud he was of me. I was excited about my degree and my new career. All the children were in school by that time, and I was ready to transition into a new life. I wanted to be a full-time nurse practitioner at the clinic and work beside Fernando. Two months after graduation, I received my license.

"I'm really excited to work in the clinic as a nurse practitioner. I can still help with the payroll and some administration, but I really want to be a provider," I told Fernando after I had received my license.

"It's my clinic. I make those decisions," he said coldly. "I don't want you there every day. I need to see what hours you can work. You don't have to work for money. I make enough."

I was shocked. "But I want to work. I studied to be a nurse practitioner. I can apply to work at another clinic."

"No. You're not working with anyone else, and you're not working full-time at the clinic. I need space in my life. I'll decide when you work and where. The children need you."

"I can work when the children are in school," I said, trying to be flexible.

"This conversation is finished," he said angrily. "Don't be high maintenance; don't start with the mental masturbation.

I'm just doing this to be supportive. I don't need you there." He walked away.

I conformed to working two days a week. I did not fight. I did not object. I followed the schedule, slowly allowing my voice and desires to be silenced. I started playing tennis and joined a team on Mondays and Wednesdays. Tennis gave me girlfriends and sanity. It kept me alive.

I made excuses for his behavior, telling myself that he was type-A personality and he was stressed at work. I felt happy in the presence of my children and my girlfriends, but I walked on eggshells around him. I was always the good wife, so much so that he started calling me Santa Pamelita.

Slowly, I slipped into the abyss. Slowly, my voice disappeared. Slowly, I became invisible.

VENICE

As the kids grew, we started taking spontaneous, unplanned trips. One Wednesday in February, Fernando came home and said, "Pack the kids' clothes. We're going to Venice for the weekend, and we leave tomorrow. I found tickets on sale for three hundred dollars, round trip. We leave at noon."

"What about school?" I asked anxiously. "What if they have tests?"

"So what? They learn more going on trips than listening to teachers. I'm taking them. I don't care what the school thinks. If I say my kids go, then they do. No school is going to give me rules. I make the rules." He laughed out loud.

"Fernando, they have homework and projects. Since you have the tickets, why don't you go by yourself?"

"I'm taking the kids. You can come or not, but they are going. Get them ready."

I stared at him, then hurried to pack. I needed to go with them. I didn't trust that he wouldn't have one of his outbursts when he was alone with the kids. So we all went.

We arrived in Venice at ten o'clock on Friday morning.

"We have to stay up, or the jet lag will get worse. Let's go eat something. It's Carnival this weekend. We can walk, eat, and go buy masks. Who wants a mask?" Fernando asked excitedly after we'd gone through customs.

"We all do, right, kids?" I said. "Let's keep on walking. If we stop, we'll fall asleep."

As we made our way through the streets of Venice, I said, "Look at the parade! It's crazy. I love the costumes. It's like Mardi Gras in Venice." I forgot my worries about school, thinking, *He is right to give them this experience.* The joy of being there filled me also.

"Papi, Papi, can I have ice cream?" Natalia asked excitedly when she saw a gelato store.

Fernando hugged the children. "Yes, as many as you can eat. Every flavor you want to try. We're on vacation. This is better than school."

We walked through the narrow streets, stopping to take pictures on all the bridges. The children had their faces painted. We bought small souvenirs, and eventually, we found a place to eat.

"What do you want to eat?" Fernando asked, smiling. "I'm not really hungry, but I am thirsty. I'll have a whiskey with ice. Order, whatever you want."

My heart sank. The children and I exchanged glances. One drink lead to another, and my chest tightened. After the first drink, his mood started to change.

"We need to go," he stated after the third drink. "Eat fast; I'm tired."

We ate hurriedly and walked silently behind him to the hotel. The Carnival was still going on, and we wanted to stay, to listen to the music and enjoy all the costumes, but we left. The next day, the scenario repeated itself. We had a lot of fun, laughing and taking pictures until three in the afternoon, when he wanted a drink.

When we returned to the hotel on the second day, I went into the children's room. It was decorated with floral wallpaper, and Venetian masks hung in the bathroom. It was a cozy space with two double beds. I gave them permission to watch movies and order room service, which excited them.

Closing the connecting door, I took a deep breath and said a silent prayer. *Please let him be asleep.* Then he screamed.

"What is your problem, you stupid woman? What did you tell the children about me? Santa Pamelita, who thinks men shouldn't have affairs. You women are all the same; you think you're smarter and better than us." He slammed the bathroom door open as he entered it, a whiskey and ice in his hand.

"Fernando, please, keep it down. The children are next door," I said loudly, looking at the connecting door.

He threw open the door and stomped toward me, grabbing my arm and screaming, "Don't you ever tell me what to do. I pay for everything; you are a princess, stupid woman. You are like my mother and my sister. Ungrateful, always causing problems."

I immediately went silent as the smell of whiskey on his breath assaulted me, a scent I had come to hate. My heart raced. I could feel the blood rushing to my head, and my legs were shaking. When he finally let go, I stumbled back into the bed. There was no place to go; I could only stay. I didn't want to disturb the children. I quickly crawled into bed, curled into a fetal position, and prayed to die. Then I remembered the kids and prayed for the strength to endure for them.

Fernando was angry at life, angry at women, angry at anyone who had ever challenged him. The rest of the weekend passed in a whirlwind, and on Sunday, we flew back to Houston.

Monday morning, I took the children to school and then met with my tennis friends.

"I can't play. I'm really tired; I have jet lag."

"Jet lag? Where have you been?" Helena asked.

"We went to Venice."

"Venice, Italy?" she asked, surprised. The four of us made our way to the courts.

"That sounds exciting and stressful at the same time," Sylvia Chavez said as she picked up her racket. "Why do you do it? Why don't you just say no?"

I looked at my friends and smiled. I felt sick to my stomach as I thought, *I'm exhausted. I'm tired. We are always on the go. And I have to go. I can't leave the kids alone with him. He changes drastically; he is kind, and then he is cruel. Jekyll or Hyde, who will I meet at night? I have to protect them. When he finally falls asleep, then I can let my guard down. It's my secret. My life, his drinking, our lies.*

The deceptions of an alcoholic family.

My friends looked at me silently, expecting a response. I laughed and changed the subject; life needed to go on. *So exciting from the outside, but a prison on the inside.*

We took trips all over the world. Trips to China, Europe, South Africa, and Latin America. Trips that were stressful due to alcohol and Fernando's outbursts of anger. I learned to read the pattern. The drinking always started on the airplane, and his paranoia would silently enter until I became his enemy in the bedroom. There would be screams and accusations. He would throw objects and break things.

I became all the women that had ever hurt him or challenged him. My daughters became his sister, who was never physically punished but instead was the quiet observer, witnessing her brother being harshly disciplined. My son, on the other hand, was a reminder of his father, a protector whom he loved. Fernando wasn't threatened by Nico.

On our trip to China, things got extremely bad. We were in the hotel room, and he had been drinking for hours. This time, I couldn't help myself. I reacted.

"You fucking crazy bitch. Who do you think you are? You live like a princess, and you think you can tell me what to do? You think you're smarter than me? You are so fucking crazy.

Mental masturbation, like all women. You are no different than the rest, always thinking you are better. You are stupid, stupid, stupid."

I answered back angrily, "Don't you call me stupid, and don't scream at me. No one has ever screamed at me before."

"Poor Pamelita, no one ever screamed at her before. She is so stupid; she thinks people don't scream. Everyone screams, Pamelita, or it won't get through your fucking head." He grabbed me by the arm harshly. I froze, as always. Realizing my mistake, I didn't answer again as I stared at his glazed eyes and beet-red face. That day, fear embraced me, and I silently retreated.

The next morning, he apologized.

"Pamelita, I'm so sorry about last night. Just don't push my buttons. If I'm angry, don't engage me. It's all your fault; I never act like this when I'm alone. I'll make it up to you and the kids. I bought you some jewelry. It's beautiful, and I'm asking for forgiveness. I would never hurt you."

"Fernando, the drinking is making you crazy. It's scary. Please stop; I'm afraid."

"Pamelita, I wouldn't be able to work if I had a drinking problem," he corrected. "It's the stress in my life that makes me crazy. Don't you ever contradict me either. I don't have a problem. Stop imagining things before I get angry." I let the conversation die.

One day, he was laughing and joking when he unexpectedly grabbed my arm and bit it forcefully. The pain made me react angrily, and I raised my voice. "Fernando, don't you ever, ever bite me again. It hurts, and it's cruel. It's not a game."

"I didn't hurt you," he screamed. "I was just playing. What is your problem? Can't you take a joke?" He grabbed my arm again, and I pulled away forcefully.

"That is not a joke; you hurt me." I turned around and left while he called me stupid and ignorant.

Alcohol, fear, tears, and laughter were our traveling companions. The last days of the trips were always followed by gifts and words of forgiveness. Whenever we returned home, I wanted to crawl into bed and sleep. Living was slowly becoming exhausting.

To counteract it, I started celebrating everything because life was easier with other people around. I planned parties and dinners to bring laughter into our home. Our friends and family would come, and alcohol would flow.

But loneliness would still engulf me when night fell and the house was empty.

THE LIES

As time passed, work, affairs, and drinking intensified. By November 2001, we had been married for twelve years. We had a lake house in Conroe where we went on weekends. Several years after the children were born, though, Fernando started going there alone on Tuesday nights. I objected in the beginning, but after a few months, I stopped opposing it.

"I don't understand why you have to leave for Conroe every Tuesday night," I would say in the beginning. "We're a family. None of my friend's husbands leave every week. Please, let's just go up on weekends."

"Pamelita, it's my mental therapy," he would say whenever the conversation came up. "I need some time alone to decompress. The clinic is very stressful. You know how hard I work. This gives me some space to relax. It's hard working all day and coming home to a family with small children. I love you all, but I need space. You could do it too, but you would need to take the kids with you. Don't leave them here."

"Fernando, the children are in school. That's not even an option. We're a family."

"Then you just have to trust me," he answered angrily one evening near the beginning of his weekly escapes. "What else do you want, princess? Don't be high maintenance; don't become a fucking bitch."

I heard all the words I wanted to answer in my head, but I couldn't speak them anymore. My vocal cords had slowly frozen.

When he was gone, it was relaxing. The children and I started planning easy meals and activities for those evenings. It was a time when I could let my guard down. We would order pizza, finish homework, and usually watch movies. It was fun to come home on Tuesdays and not have to pick up everything. To not have to worry about mood swings.

One Tuesday night in November, I put the children to bed early. I was filing papers in the study when I saw a credit card statement with my name on it. It had charges I hadn't made. I looked at the credit card number, but I didn't recognize it. My heart started pounding, and my hands were sweating. I knew what it meant: there was another woman.

I ran upstairs to our bedroom, opened his closet, and started looking for any proof of an affair. I was shaking as I went through the drawers. Hidden under folded sweaters, I found cards and notes with no signature, all written by another woman.

In a panic, I called a friend and told her I had an emergency. I asked if she could please come stay with my children. She agreed, and I left the house at ten at night to drive to Conroe. When I arrived, I pulled up quietly, expecting to find him there. I opened the door to find that the house was dark. There was no movement; it was empty. I ran through all the bedrooms and finally sat on the floor, the phone shaking in my hands.

I made the call.

The phone rang several times with no answer, but I didn't give up. I called again and again. Eventually, he picked up.

"Why are you calling at midnight?" he asked groggily. "I was asleep. What's going on?"

"Where are you?" I screamed, my voice trembling.

"I'm in Conroe, sleeping. You woke me up." I could tell he was more awake. His voice was on edge.

"Where are you? Who are you with? You are not in Conroe; I'm here. Where are you?"

There was silence for a few minutes.

"You need to calm down," he finally said emphatically. "I had an emergency, so I'm at the hospital. I had to drive back."

"You're lying, and you know it. Why, why? What have you done?" I started sobbing. He hung up the phone, and I couldn't reach him again. I drove back to Houston at three in the morning.

When I arrived, I found my friend sleeping on the sofa. I thanked her and told her I couldn't talk but that I would reach out to her in the morning. Once she left, I went to my room. I crawled into bed, set my alarm for six, and fell asleep. I was numb. When the alarm went off, my head was pounding, I got up. I tried to fix the children breakfast, but I was moving slowly and my hands were shaking. I wasn't laughing and talking like I usually did in the morning.

Christina looked at me and asked, "Mami, what's happening?"

"Your dad is having an affair. I found out last night. He wasn't at the lake." I didn't think about it; I just blurted it out. I was hurting.

She fixed her eyes on mine. Then she got up, went to the pantry, and took out Pop-Tarts, putting them in the toaster.

Then she turned to her siblings. "We're having Pop-Tarts for breakfast. Mami, you sit down; we'll take over."

We all ate in silence. They were ten, nine, and six years old. They got dressed, and I drove them to school before driving to the clinic. I walked in and went to his office. He hadn't arrived yet. I looked at his desk: everything was in order, everything was locked. I looked for something. I picked up the phone and started calling about the charges on the credit card statement I had found. While I was doing this, a staff member came into the office and asked me if I needed any help.

Looking at her, I asked, "Is the doctor having an affair?"

She froze. We both knew she couldn't answer me directly or she would lose her job. She stared at me, then lowered her head.

"Is it the blonde?" I asked.

She nodded and looked at the wall. "I'm sorry." She stood in the same place for several minutes, then walked away. No words could take away the pain I felt at that moment of confirmation. Memories filled my mind. The other woman's son was friends with Nicholas, and the realization made me angry. It reminded me of my father trying to make me befriend his girlfriend. I realized, too, that something about her had always made me uncomfortable. Fernando had always spoken derogatorily about her, yet he would also defend her fiercely.

Exhaustion overtook me. I went to my office and waited.

After what seemed like an eternity, he walked into the clinic.

He saw me but didn't acknowledge me. He walked into his office, and I followed. He slammed the door behind me. When I repeated the question I'd asked the nurse, he screamed, accusing me of making up stories. I showed him the credit card statements, the cards, and all the other proof I had. He ripped them from my hands and stormed around.

"Leave my office. Leave my office now! You are fired. I'll get a restraining order if you ever step back in here. I will destroy you and keep the children. You're making up lies. You fucking liar."

My face burned, and my legs started to shake. I felt like hitting him. Anger filled me and I wanted to lash out, but I just walked out. I headed toward the lab and picked up everything I knew belonged to her. I grabbed scissors and cut up all her pictures. I wanted to destroy her. I was angry and hurting. Betrayal had entered my world. There had been signs, there had been gossip, but denial had filled my mind.

Leaving the clinic, I got in the car and drove to the closest church, Our Lady of Walsingham. I sat in the pew and cried inconsolably until I fell asleep. I was woken one or two hours later by one of the priests. Seeing that I was hurting, he listened to my story and prayed with me. I had a flashback to my childhood: my mom crying on her bed as my father screamed at her, denying that he was having an affair. My father had convinced me later that it was all lies, and I had believed him. The priest's prayer gave me a sense of peace in that moment and the strength to drive back home.

On my way home, I started calling the few friends I still had. Everyone gave me different advice.

"Fight for your marriage; turn a blind eye."

"Leave; don't stay. I'll find an attorney for you."

"Be strong for the children. Children need their parents together."

"Stay; he'll get over it. Affairs lose their power once they're discovered."

"He'll always have them. You need to leave."

"All men have affairs. Just ignore it until it goes away."

I was in a state of confusion. Humiliation, betrayal, sadness, anger, and loss all swam through me, and my head was pounding as I drove to pick up the children from school. They sensed it had been a rough day for. As they climbed into the car, I took out our happy notebook.

"Okay, guys, what was the happiest thing that happened today?" I asked once they had all climbed in and had their seatbelts on.

"Mami, Mami," Nico squealed excitedly. "Maggie gave me a Starburst. That means she really likes me."

"Make sure you write that down," I told him as I continued driving. "Christy, Natis, what about you? Something good happens every day."

This notebook had been our routine for years. Eventually, the pattern would move to the dinner table.

We went home, and they started doing homework. I got a phone call from the clinic.

"He's going home," the office manager said, her voice agitated. "We've never seen him as angry as he is today. Please protect yourself. You can't be home alone with him." She hung up before I could respond.

Fear gripped me, and I told the children, "We can't sleep here today. Papi is really angry. Let's get your clothes for tomorrow. We have to leave now."

I hurriedly packed their school clothes, and we left. I drove around for a while, looking for a hotel. I didn't want one close to our house. I stopped at a hotel on the feeder road of Highway 59, and we went inside to get a room.

"I need a room with two double beds for the night."

"I'll need your name and a credit card," the receptionist said without looking up.

"No name, please. I'll pay cash. We just need a place for one night." I looked around the hotel lobby anxiously, making sure I hadn't been followed.

The receptionist, an older black lady, lifted her gaze from computer screen. She looked at me and then at the children. Glancing at me again, I could see understanding in her face. The kindness in her eyes gave me courage.

I will always remember how she smiled then and said, "I'll give you a name. Jane Austen. Have you eaten?" She glanced at the children.

"No, we left in a hurry."

"The kitchen is closed, but I'll send you cookies and milk for the children."

I thanked her profusely for helping us. Before I left, she added, "I'll pray for you and the children."

I turned around to the children. "You can finish your homework here, and I'll take you to school tomorrow."

"What's going to happen to Papi, Mami?" six-year-old Natalia asked.

"He'll be okay. We'll be safer here tonight," I answered, trying to reassure her.

The cookies and milk arrived, and they finished their homework. The noise of the TV filled the silence of the room. No one was really watching, but it helped calm their anxiety. Eventually, the cell phone started ringing. I didn't answer for the first hour, and the calling continued. Natalia started begging me to answer.

"Please, Mami, what if it's Papi and he wants us home?"

I finally picked up the phone, hesitantly.

"Where are you? Where are the children?" He sounded anxious, but I could tell he had been drinking. His voice was slurred.

"We won't be coming home tonight," I answered. "I can't tell you where we are, but we're okay."

"Please come home. I love you, and I love the kids. It's over. It's over. It didn't mean anything. I need you and the children." He was crying.

I put the phone down and looked at the children. They hadn't said much all evening. They were like robots, following my orders.

"Tomorrow we'll go home." Relief filled their faces.

In the morning, I took them to school and then drove home. As I entered, I saw Fernando on the sofa, waiting for me.

"It's done. It's over. I'm sorry. You and the children are my life. I can't live without you. I already fired her. I don't want a scandal at the clinic." He smiled and tried to kiss me, but I turned my face away from him. "I'll make it up to you and the kids. I promise I will. I never want to hurt you again."

I wanted to believe him. I couldn't forget the lost looks on my children's faces.

"I don't want you at the clinic. It's too disruptive right now. You can come back later, but not now." His voice was soft as he reached out to touch me.

"What about my job?" I asked.

He gripped my hand. "You don't need it right now. I make the money, not you. The kids need you, and I want us to work this out. This is the best decision. We're a family."

"Can we go to counseling together? I think it would really help us."

"Pamelita, we don't need counseling," he said, brushing it off kindly, without anger. "I just had an affair. It doesn't mean anything. You're my wife. It was just a game. Everyone has an affair. But it's over now. We have a family."

A knot had formed in my stomach, but I wanted to believe it was over. I knew he was lying, but I believed my own lies that things would get better.

I had lost my job. My husband had had an affair. My life was spiraling downward, and I didn't know how to stop it. I ran upstairs and vomited. I lay in bed and slept for several hours. When I woke up, it was time to go pick the children up from school. They were happy to see me.

"Mom, can we go home today?" Nicholas asked hopefully.

"Yes, we will. Papi and I are going to try to work this out."

"I don't want you to get a divorce," Natalia stated. "I have friends whose parents are divorced."

"We won't. It's going to be okay." I felt like I was making the right decision.

I drove home with the children, and as the door opened, they ran inside the house, happy to be back home. He was home expecting them, and the house was full of flowers and balloons. He hugged them and kissed them excitedly and started talking about a trip to China he was planning for all of us. Their little faces beamed with happiness.

The next day, after leaving the kids at school, I went to visit my friend Anne Davis. As I talked, she listened; there was no judgment, only acceptance. She gave no advice; she only encouraged me to be strong and made me promise that I would come to her house next time, rather than a hotel. I told her I hoped there would never be a next time.

Two years earlier, my mother had moved in with us, and we had built an apartment for her in the garage. That afternoon, as we arrived home after school, Natalia ran to me anxiously.

"Mami, Mami, where is Grandma's furniture?" she asked breathlessly.

I stared at her and then ran to the garage apartment. I opened the door and started screaming.

"Mom, Mom! Where are you?"

I ran desperately through the house, opening every bedroom door in hopes of finding her. I went out into the yard, screaming as I desperately looked for her. The children followed me, also searching for her.

"Mom, Mom, where are you? Where are you?"

I finally collapsed in the yard, crying, and curled into a fetal position. The children huddled beside me. I couldn't stop crying. After what seemed like an eternity — but was probably only minutes — the housekeeper who had been there that day sat on the ground beside me and told me what had happened.

"After you left for work today, he called the gardener and me to come pack all your mother's things into black garbage bags. He told us to put them out in the driveway. We had to obey; he pays our checks every week.

"When your mother came, she was in shock. She also cried and cried. She called your brother. He came for her and her things. Everything was moved."

I hadn't seen my brother in several weeks, and after that, it would be another eight years before I had any kind of contact with him or his family again. Juan and Elsa were living a nightmare with him at work; I was living a nightmare with him at home. Nightmares we never shared.

"I am sorry," the housekeeper continued. "There was nothing we could do. He told us he would fire us if we called you. We just followed his rules. I'm so sorry, *Señora. Perdónenos. Teníamos que hacerlo. Era como un loco. Perdón, Señora.*" There were tears in her eyes by the time she finished.

I stared at her in disbelief before finally getting up. My heart was broken. I couldn't speak for days afterward. I didn't have words. I couldn't feel anything. I was so numb. Every feeling and every emotion was dead.

Looking back, I can still remember the pain I felt for not having the courage to stand up to him that day. For years afterward, I would ask myself how I could have allowed that to happen and still continue with him. But I realize now that abuse creeps into a person's life, taking them slowly to the slaughterhouse without their awareness.

Domestic abuse is not just the bruised, black eyes of a woman who has been beaten. It's the small cuts that occur daily from which their life eventually bleeds out. It is the isolation they endure and the words that, one by one, strip away human dignity. It's the intimidation of continual threats to take away the children or to leave the victim in the streets. It's power and control over another human being.

That day, my spirit broke, and I totally lost my voice, lost my strength, and lost my path. It would take me years to regain my strength and my voice and to walk away.

He came home that evening with Colombian food and presents for the children. We ate in front of the TV, watching *Yo soy Betty, la fea*, a famous Colombian telenovela. I couldn't speak, and he pretended I was invisible. All his attention was for the kids alone. He wouldn't look me in the eyes.

I didn't eat for days. I only drank tea and water. My mother was gone, and I had lost my voice.

Slowly over the weeks that followed, the children helped me come out of the deep hole I had fallen into. It was over between Fernando and me, but I still didn't leave. I did, however, visit a divorce attorney in the month that followed. She had been highly recommended by a girlfriend and was everything I wasn't at that point in my life. She was a fighter: assertive and out for blood. I left the office with her card and never went back. I didn't have the strength for that battle. Getting out of bed everyday was already hard enough.

Over the next four years, the abuse escalated, and we were totally isolated from family, friends, and coworkers. There were verbal and physical outbursts. If words didn't hurt enough, he performed cruel jokes, like biting, pulling our hair, or putting gum in our hair. He would laugh and then get angry if someone protested.

He would drink; we would run and hide.

The affairs continued, both with other women and with alcohol, yet I didn't leave. It destroyed our family, and ultimately, alcohol would take his life. But it didn't happen overnight; it took years, and it slowly affected us all.

Slowly, my marriage had become a quartet: Alcohol, Fear, Fernando, and me. While Alcohol was Fernando's companion, Fear had become mine.

Life was calm until Alcohol joined us with the first drink of the day. Sometimes it was noon, sometimes later in the evening. When Alcohol joined Fernando, Fear joined me. I was afraid to disturb him, afraid of his reactions, afraid of what he might do to me or to the children. I never knew what was going to happen once he had a drink in his hands.

I began my own battle to remove Alcohol from our home, but it was not easy. We had built a special place for him, with beautiful paneled shelving and glass doors, which we had stocked with a variety of alcohol, from whiskey to wine, to rum and vodka. Now I wanted Alcohol gone. I would pour him down the drain, mark the whisky bottle every night to see how much Fernando had consumed, pour water into the bottle to dilute the whiskey, and throw bottles of wine in the garbage can, covering them with trash so they would go unnoticed.

But as bottles disappeared, they were replaced the next day. Nothing seemed to help. I was walking on tiptoe, afraid to wake the lion.

I knew then that Alcohol would never leave us, and if he was around, Fear would stay.

The children and I learned to hide in our own house. We knew the bedroom he couldn't find, the closet he wouldn't open, and the bed we could fit under. Christina's room became our haven since it was downstairs. At night, Fernando, along with his silent companion poured into a cut-glass tumbler, would be in the study reading or watching TV. The children and I would be upstairs, doing homework silently, until we would hear him calling for us or screaming his mother's name.

One night after dinner, the children and I went to the game room to work on homework. He stayed downstairs, watching *Forrest Gump*. Everything was peaceful and quiet for about an hour. Then he began screaming. "Teresa, Teresa, where are you hiding? I know you're making up stories about me." The children turned around and stared at me, their faces tensing up as fear came into their eyes.

"Mami, why is he calling for our grandmother?" Christina asked, confused. "She's not even here."

"He must have reached the scene that always upsets him. It's the one where Jenny is hiding from her father. You keep doing your homework. I'm going to check on him before he comes up," I said, trying to remain calm.

As I entered the hallway, I saw him coming up the stairs. His face was flushed, and he looked at me suspiciously. He wasn't alone; Alcohol was a step behind him.

"Why are you hiding the children? Why aren't you answering when I call you?" he screamed as he reached for me. I could see Alcohol's shadow lurking behind him, laughing invisibly. For him, this was a game. For me, it was survival.

Fernando pulled my hair, and I grabbed his hand, screaming. "Let go! Don't pull my hair; that hurts!"

His eyes were glazed, confused, and he released his grip and started laughing.

"You can't do that," I said angrily, backing away from him. "It hurts, and it's not funny."

"You always exaggerate. It's just for fun. Children, come give me a hug. Mami always gets mad for nothing; she can't take a joke."

"Leave them alone. Run, kids," I screamed. "Run, go hide!"

"Papi, we have too much homework to do," Christina said, grabbing her siblings. They scattered fast, one by one, and I followed them downstairs into Christina's room.

The alcohol made him stumble, preventing him from moving as fast as us. It gave us time to lock the door. We all climbed into the one bed and started praying the Rosary together.

"Jesus, protect us. Hail Mary, full of grace, the Lord is with thee . . ."

"That stupid school," he shouted as he stumbled toward the bedroom. "You don't have to do everything the teacher says. You're the boss. No one is going to make my children work like slaves. Tomorrow, I'm going to call the director to tell her this is abuse."

We heard him pounding on the door and screaming. Eventually, there was silence. We knew the drill. Remain quiet, and eventually we could come out because he would have retreated to his room and fallen asleep.

It wasn't long before I heard him snoring and we had peace.

I tried to find words to discuss the overconsumption of alcohol with Fernando, but it was never easy. One Friday, he took the day off to work on his investment papers. I felt this was the right time. We were both alone in the house, and I made a pot of coffee.

"Fernando, I wanted to talk to you about something that's concerning me," I began.

"What is it, Pamelita? What is it now?" He sighed and grabbed his cup of coffee, looking annoyed. He never wanted to discuss feelings.

"I believe you're drinking too much. It's affecting our life, our marriage, our family." I watched him cautiously as I spoke, hoping he would hear me before he poured his first whiskey of the day.

"I can stop any time I want. Don't you tell me I'm drinking to much; it's just a glass of whiskey a day. I don't see it affecting me at all. You're always trying to act saintly. I will never, ever have a problem. Do you understand? Don't you ever say I have a drinking problem. If I had a drinking problem, I wouldn't be able to go to work, stupid lady."

He stated this angrily in a loud voice as he paced the room, the cup of coffee in his hand. His face was flushed.

"I just want you to be careful," I said, lowering my voice and looking away. "I'm sorry I said anything. I love you, and I'm just worried."

"Don't you ever challenge me again. You don't know anything. I have given you everything. You know how hard I work. I only take a drink to relax at night. I can stop whenever I want."

I listened quietly as the topic was closed. There was nothing I could say that would make a difference. Alcohol already had a hold on his life, having become his best friend. I looked at my watch and realized it was time to leave. Sadness wrapped its arms around me; I was losing hope.

"I need to go pick the children up from school and take them snacks. It's a late night for us today. They have piano lessons and soccer." I picked up the car keys. I was frustrated that my words had not been heard, and my stomach was in knots. I hoped the failed conversation would not have negative effects later that day.

It was eight o'clock at night by the time we returned home. I stared down the driveway through darkness, the same darkness that had entered my world. This was where the children had learned to ride their bikes and how to skate. It was where we used to have cars parked for family celebrations, where I had broken down and cried when Mom left. This driveway held so many memories of laughter, tears, and family secrets.

I fixed my eyes on the house in the distance, so close, yet so far away. When we had arrived at the gate and put the code in, the gate refused to open. Our home had become unattainable with the simple locking of the gate.

Why is he doing this now? He's pushing us away, yet I don't want to be pushed away. I want a normal family; I want him to fight for our family. Why does he lock us out? Why? Dear Lord, help me; I feel so alone.

I tried to get it open several times before I turned to the children. "Nicholas, see if you can push the gate open enough for you to get through."

"It's pretty tight, Mami."

"It's the only way for us to get in. You have to go open the front door and put the code in."

"You know he locked us out again," Christina said. "Why does he do that?"

"He turned off the power and went to sleep," I said anxiously. "We need to get in the house to turn it back on."

"I've got it, Mami. Just wait here. I know what to do." Nicholas ran to the front door.

Five minutes later, the gate opened, and we drove in. When we walked into the house, all the lights were turned off. It was only eight o'clock at night, but it felt more like midnight. I went upstairs to my bedroom and found him sleeping. I left him alone. There was a sense of peace at night when he was sleeping. I helped the children get their things ready for the morning and tucked them into bed. I felt a deep sense of loneliness as I did. I was battling Alcohol and losing.

One evening, we had friends over for a barbecue. This had become a rare occasion in our life. Alcohol can make people obnoxious, and slowly friends stop coming over. That particular day, we were outside, and my girlfriend Luz Maria Mejia looked me in the eyes and said gently, "I have something I want you to read. I think it's important."

"I love everything you share with me. What is it?" I smiled enthusiastically as she gave me two printed pages.

I took them and read the title: "Warning Signs of Alcoholism." As I stared at the paper, a cold chill ran through my body. *How does she know? Nobody knows what happens at night. Dear God, please, I don't want people to know.* Deep down inside, I knew she was right, but I couldn't get myself to admit it to her. I smiled and thanked her.

"I'll read it later tonight. I don't want him to see the title."

I hid it for later. Luz Maria became my walking partner. She never asked about Fernando, but she was always inquiring about the children and offering ideas of ways to help them. Her words were gentle reminders that I wasn't alone. She was an angel in disguise.

Alcohol taught us to lie to ourselves. Fernando learned to believe he didn't have a problem. I told myself it would get better. Alcohol smiled as we both put our masks on during the day. At night, as the masks fell off.and alcohol accompanied us, we suffered as a family. We convinced ourselves of the lies as a way to survive.

Our children attended Catholic schools, yet religion and God couldn't be mentioned in the house, or rage would take him over. I hid every Bible for fear of upsetting him.

One night, we watched the newly released movie *Evita*, featuring Madonna and Antonio Banderas. There was a scene in which Evita was about ten years old and her father had just died. She was not allowed to go to the funeral because her mother had been the father's mistress.

Fernando got angry and started screaming at the TV. "What is wrong with the fucking aristocracy? It was her father; she needs to be able to go. He made her a bastard; she didn't have a choice."

I remained silent and kept my eyes on the screen. *Please hurry up, scene. Get his mind off the funeral. Let the music begin so we can watch the rest of the movie.* When that took too long, I got up from the couch. "Kids, who wants to help me make popcorn?"

"All of us do, Mami," Nicholas stated, jumping up from the sofa and getting his sisters to follow him to the kitchen. "Why is Papi so upset at the movie?" he asked innocently.

"It reminds him of his childhood, Nico. Let's make the popcorn and go back to finish the movie," I said hurriedly, trying to brush away the incident.

At the end of the movie, Evita is dying, and there is a crucifix at her bedside. Fernando went into a rage and started throwing books at the screen. We all sat quietly, pretending we didn't see the explosion of anger.

I was exhausted during the day for the nights were living nightmares. My heart raced with palpitations, and I prayed to die every night. *God, please let me go home to you, but not unless my children will be all right.*

Social isolation had become a part of our life. If anyone crossed him, questioned him about erratic behavior, or called him out on his cruel jokes or affairs, they were marked off the list of his friends. He had a mental list of people he knew, and slowly most of them were deleted. Little by little, we became alone in our isolated island.

Fernando believed everyone was out to get him, and we believed him. His paranoia was a disease that had poisoned the whole family. Night after night, with Alcohol by his side, he was haunted by the ghosts of his past.

AWAKENING

Our life had become empty. There was little communication between us: the children and I laughed together during the day, but we were silent at night. Nights were dreaded, filled with anxiety. I started having panic attacks.

One day, I broke the silence. I started asking questions about certain behaviors. I had forgotten what was normal.

"Is it normal to receive flowers after we had to leave the house and sleep in a hotel anonymously night before? Is he truly sorry, or is it abnormal?"

"Pam, that's not normal," answered Nancy, a tennis friend and social worker. "It's abuse. You are afraid of him. He tells you you can't do anything right. He has isolated you from your family and friends. He tells you he'll take the children away from you. These are signs, and there are many more.

"You are the only one who can break that cycle. No one can do it for you. You get nervous if you don't answer the phone the first time it rings when it's him. You walk on eggshells around him. You've stopped doing anything with us, you're so scared to leave the children at night. You aren't the woman I met five years ago. If you die, the kids will die with you.

"But you have your girlfriends and your mother. Please hear us. He tells you everyday that you are alone and you are stupid and ugly, but we love you. The children need you. He is sick, Pam, and you can't fight mental illness and alcoholism."

Nancy said all of this quietly while looking me in the eyes.

There was pain, hurt, anger, and isolation. In the mornings, Fernando had no recollection of the previous evening. The blackouts had begun.

"Do you remember last night?" I would ask.

"Not really. What happened?" As he listened, he would cover his face with his hands.

"You started throwing books at me," I would say. "You chased us until we had to lock ourselves in Christina's room. We can't live like this anymore. You need help."

"I'm so sorry. You know that's not me. I love you and the kids. I would never hurt you," he would answer, but I no longer believed him.

Another chaotic night followed by flowers. I prayed for guidance, yet I felt like I was walking in darkness. I prayed for miracles as my life crumbled around me. I was so afraid of life; I had stopped living and had started dying inside. I couldn't understand Isaiah 41:10 – "Fear not for I am with you: be not dismayed; I am your God" – for I lived in fear and I was exhausted.

My physical health deteriorated. I lost fifteen pounds and had trouble keeping food down. My children were sad and angry.

I went to Alcoholics Anonymous meetings twice, but I made the mistake of not hiding the handouts. When Fernando saw them, he became enraged and tore them into small pieces, screaming and asking me if I had gone crazy or if I was an imbecile.

I never went back.

I called a number for an intervention and asked his family members to help.

"I need help," I said when I made the call. "My husband's drinking is out of control. I'm afraid all the time. He won't admit he has a problem and refuses help."

"Lady, thank you for calling. We will try to help. Let me explain how this program works. We need the family and close friends to be involved and supportive if we go to pick him up. The family and close friends need to be there to tell him they love him and that he needs help. Do you think you can get the support?"

"I don't know if that will work. Nobody knows what it's like at night. I'll try. I'll call back."

I put the phone down and sat on the bed. *There is no way he won't find out if I call them. He needs help, and he's bringing us down with him. They won't believe me; it's just a drink or two at night, they'll say. What should I do? Is it really worth it? But if they pick him up and he can get treatment, he may accept it. Or maybe not.*

I stared blankly, hopeless, and my heart felt heavy. I looked around the bedroom—the king-size bed, the modern light-beige furniture, the large windows looking out on the backyard. Nothing mattered anymore. This felt like my last call for help. I took a deep breath and hesitantly picked up the phone. I dialed once, then hung up before the second ring. I took another deep breath and dialed again.

I called his sister first. "Hello. How are you doing? I wanted to talk to you about Fernando," I said hopefully.

"What's up with my brother?" she asked. "I haven't talked to him in a while. Is he doing okay?"

"Do you remember a year ago, when you visited, how we talked about his alcohol consumption?"

Silence filled the other end of the line. Finally, she said, "Yes, I do. What does this phone call have to do with that?"

"The problem is worse. I want to get him into treatment, but I can't do it alone. You would have to be here, and they would come pick him up with all of us present. He would feel loved and supported."

"No. No, you can't ask me to do that. He doesn't drink that much, and I would never do that. How could you even think of such an idea after everything he has given you? I can't believe you're that ungrateful." She hung up before I could say anything else.

I was left feeling empty, but it was what I had expected. The next phone call would be my last. It was a phone call to Colombia, to Fernando's best friend growing up. I was more hopeful, but I had forgotten they were drinking buddies.

"Do you think you could come? He needs help. The alcohol has taken over his life. I want to put him in a treatment center, but I need you here before that can happen. He needs to know we all support him."

"You're crazy. Who would do such a thing? No, I would never do that to him. He doesn't drink that much. He's just having fun with friends. Who cares if he gets drunk? Maybe you need help, but not him. By the way, I'm going to tell him about this conversation; he's my best friend." He hung up before I could say another word.

I froze as fear embraced me again. I knew he would call Fernando right away. *How could I have even thought about asking for his help?* My head began to pound. I ran and vomited up the contents of my stomach—something that happened more frequently and uncontrollably as I lost my voice.

I prepared for the screams and the anger. They came that night, and I remained silent. Fernando called me to the study, and as I went, I silently prayed, *Protect me, Lord. Protect me.* I was a sheep going to the slaughterhouse, walking slowly to my death.

"You're lying. You're making up stories. Carlos called me today and told me you had called him to come to the States so I could be taken to a rehabilitation center. Are you fucking crazy? You, with your mental masturbation, are making up stories that

I have a drinking problem. Do you think I could go to work and get up in the mornings if I was an alcoholic? Stupid woman." He threw several books, trying to hit me as he screamed at me. I quickly ducked and remained on alert, ready to run away.

"And I read the letter you gave me last week," he added. "And it's lies, lies, all lies. I want you to read it out loud so I can tell you how wrong you are. I want you to know how stupid and insignificant you are. I have given you everything. Everything, you have everything you need. I don't care about your feelings or your emotions. It's just another case of female masturbation, like my mother making things up, making my life hell. I do what I want to do and when I want to do it."

He waved a letter I had written to him, shoving it in my face. "I said read it," he screamed, his face getting redder and his voice louder.

"Fernando," I read in a hushed voice, holding the letter in my shaking hands. "I can't talk to you, so I'm writing to you." He started getting closer to me, his rage uncontrollable.

"You're a liar. Liar!" he screamed in rage.

I took the letter, tore it in pieces, and swallowed it. I left the room, ran to the bathroom, and vomited. He pounded at the door, but I kept it locked. I crouched on the floor until there was silence—perhaps minutes, perhaps longer. I just sat and wept. I was trapped by fear.

I wrote and wrote. Writing became my solace, my voice, a silent whisper for help left unheard by anyone but by myself. When he found my diaries, he went into rage and accused me of making up stories. I swallowed crumpled paper to hide my words when he found them. Silence and fatigue filled me, a fatigue that slowly set in and stayed with me.

One day in August 2004, my mother called me and asked me to take her to her doctor's appointment. I still saw my mother weekly at the children's school, and we tried to meet elsewhere outside the house. When we arrived at her appointment, my mother introduced me to Dr. Halpern, her primary care physician. "This is my daughter, Pam. The one I've told you about. I'm worried about her health. I'll wait outside." Mom came over and kissed my forehead. "It's safe."

As my mom left the room, there was silence.

"Do you know why you're here? Why your mom asked me to see you?" Dr. Halpern asked gently.

"I'm losing weight and exhausted all the time," I answered quietly.

"Do you think you could be depressed?" she asked, taking my vital signs.

"Perhaps. I don't know. I'm just tired, always tired, and I can barely keep food down," I answered.

"Tell me about your day. What's your routine? How do you sleep?"

Slowly and gently, she continued asking questions, many questions. I started talking; I started crying. She asked, and I answered. Secrets slowly poured out in that doctor's room. She didn't write anything down in front of me; she simply sat and listened as I spilled my heart.

"Pam, you're depressed. I want you to try an antidepressant for a few months. If it helps, you'll notice changes in your mood and you'll sleep better. Let's meet weekly. It doesn't mean you're crazy. My plan is to keep you on for a year or two, and then we can wean you off. I will also recommend a counselor to work with you. It's all baby steps, but if you agree, we can work together." Dr. Halpern smiled as I nodded in agreement.

I saw Dr. Halpern weekly, and with her guidance, I developed a plan to leave Fernando. I needed to find an attorney, and I needed to save money. One of my tennis friends suggested that whenever I went to the grocery store, I should also take out cash. Weekly, I started saving cash under the mattress in my bedroom. Small bills eventually became a growing savings.

I asked my friend Anne Davis for a key to her house, something she had offered many times. I made photocopies of my diplomas, my nursing license, my driver's license, and all our passports and had Anne keep them safe.

Every week, Dr. Halpern saw me. Our appointments ran ten to fifteen minutes long, but there was always something for me to do or learn. She always had a sentence for me to memorize: "I am intelligent." "I am useful to society." "I love myself." "I am brave." Every day, I was to repeat a particular sentence throughout the day until we met again. Baby steps allowed me to finally make the choice to file for divorce five months later. I will always be grateful for Dr. Halpern and her guidance.

FINDING COURAGE

One day in November 2004, I called Anne and asked her to meet me for lunch in a small Thai restaurant in Sugar Land. When we arrived, I hugged her.

"Anne, you and I have talked about going to an attorney. I'm ready, but I don't want to go alone. Can you make an appointment for me, and could you please go with me? I need to do it now. Fernando has been cleaning the rifles in his closet every night. He sits on the floor crying, saying his life isn't worth it. I'm scared he might try to kill himself and kill us too. I hid the rifles in the attic today, but you know he'll be furious when he looks for them and can't find them."

"I've already spoken with Mr. Curry, the attorney," Anne said, holding my hands and looking me in the eye. "I called him up personally. I've known him for years; his daughter, Karen, is one of my best friends. I told him I had a friend who was going to file for divorce and wanted his information. He knows the situation you're living in, and he's waiting for us to make an appointment. And I'll go with you.

"Now let's order something, and we'll discuss it. You've done all you can."

We ate lunch and talked. There was a hint of peace entering my world again. I hugged her as we parted ways. Before I got in the car to leave, I turned around and said, "I love you, Anne. Thank you for always being there for me."

Later that evening, I got a phone call from Anne. "Pam, we have an appointment in two days, at 9:00 a.m. sharp. I know you can do it. We'll go together." She sounded confident.

"I'm ready, Anne," I answered peacefully. "It's time. I've waited enough. Nothing changes; it only gets worse."

When the attorney said he would serve Fernando the papers the next week, I froze, panicking. "Mr. Curry, why do you want to serve him at the clinic?"

"Pam, that's the way it's done. What do you want to do? I thought we were ready." He spoke patiently, trying to understand my hesitancy.

"I need to tell him first in person. I need to be prepared for his reaction. Once I tell him, you can get the papers to him."

"I understand. He will be extremely angry. But they're never prepared for this, no matter what has happened. Phone me when you've told him, and we'll get the papers to him."

The next evening, I walked into the study, where he was watching TV and drinking whiskey on the rocks. Alcohol was already present in the room, comfortably keeping him company and eyeing me suspiciously. I took a deep breath and prayed, *Jesus, I trust you.*

"Fernando, I want a divorce." I stared directly into his eyes. I was saying the words that, for year, I had only dreamed I would have the courage to say. He stared at me in disbelief.

"What did you just say?"

"I want a divorce. I can't do it any longer. We're both unhappy. The women, the drinking, your choice of friends. We're all dying together. It's toxic. This house is not a home anymore." My voice was strong; I could hear it. I said the words slowly and shakily in the beginning, but as I heard them out loud, I found the strength to continue.

I felt his anger rising, and I couldn't move. I was suddenly paralyzed with fear. He started screaming. "I'll keep the kids.

You have no money. You have no job. You'll be in the streets. Without me, you will never survive."

In my head, I repeated his words. *I have no money of my own. I don't have a job. I got fired from the office after discovering your affair. I need to survive, but you're slowly killing me.* Panic took over my body. My heart raced, my legs began trembling, and I could feel the blood rushing through my body. It was fight or flight, adrenaline rushing all over.

I ran out of the study, and he followed me, screaming. I ran to the garage apartment and hid in the closet. I could hear him screaming as my heart continued to beat uncontrollably, pounding against my chest. I took deep breaths to slow it. I was tired of hiding.

I finally came out of the closet after about forty-five minutes and found him sitting in the study with a glass of whiskey. He stared at me, his eyes glassy, his look frozen, the alcohol in his hand keeping him company.

"How could you do this to me after all I've done for you?" he asked angrily, staring directly into my eyes. "I'll tell the kids it's your fault. You asked for the divorce. You destroyed our family."

"We need to live in separate homes," I said, trying to sound convincing. "The children and I need to stay here, and you need to find another place to live until the divorce is done. I already have an attorney."

I saw the look in his eyes then. I had become his enemy. I looked at him, looked at the glass in his hand, and then walked away. I knew it would only get worse in the days to come, but I had finally said the words "I want a divorce" and something inside me had seen a glimpse of light in the future. Fernando didn't grasp the pain the children and I had lived. The abuse that had started many years ago had escalated. Abuse present

through generations, it wouldn't stop until it had been acknowledged. Abuse that led to pain and drinking. My attorney had
said I needed to stay in the house, and Fernando needed to
move out. But he wouldn't hear it.

"This is my house. If you want to leave, go and find a place
under the bridge. I'll remove you from the checking accounts,
and I'll cancel your credit card. Go see what you can do. You'll
come back begging me for forgiveness." He stared at me hate-
fully.

That evening, he locked the children in the study to tell them
the news. "Your mother has asked for a divorce. She has destroyed
our family. Your mother can leave, and we'll stay together in
this house."

Christina gathered her siblings close. "Papi, this is between
you and Mom. Don't get us involved in this. We love you both."
She stood up, opened the door of the study and walked out, her
siblings following her.

The next day, I discovered I was without a checkbook and
without a credit card. All our financial information was hidden
and locked away. My signature had been forged, and all my
accounts had been closed. I remained in the house, hoping he
would find an apartment, but he stayed. He was paying the
bills.

In the next two months, I dialed 911 during our fights whenever he would run and throw objects at me during his rages.
Nothing was done to me physically; there were no bruises on
my body.

In February, I decided the children and I needed to leave.
Sleepless nights and exhaustion had followed my declaration.
More anger built up. How could we stay in the same house?

We couldn't.

ANGELS

My girlfriends were there for me over the years, sometimes physically present, sometimes silently praying for me. I met Ana Cecilia Gonzalez, in June 1989 when she was a twenty-four-year-old cardiology patient at Texas Children's Hospital. She was in the ICU, and I was her nurse. Every year she came to Houston for her checkup, she stayed with our family. Year after year, she witnessed the changes. In November 2003, she came to visit, and I clearly remember our conversation one evening as we sat in the living room.

"Pamela, I'm leaving my husband and moving to Puebla, Mexico." At the time, she had been living in Monterrey, Mexico.

"Ana, how are you going to support yourself?" I asked. "I thought things were better between you all. I think about leaving often, but I'm still here."

"Your marriage is not the same," she said lovingly. "You have to find the courage to let go. It's killing you and the children. He has a deep problem, and you can't keep trying to help him. This is his battle, not yours."

"I don't know if I can, Ana," I said quietly. "I really don't know."

"You'll find the strength; I know you will." Her words brought tears to my eyes. I felt trapped, yet I desperately wanted out.

Hers was a story of resilience that encouraged me to find my voice. She was born with a single ventricle and transposition of the great vessels. Her parents were told she wouldn't survive past childhood. When she was eight years old, she found out she could die any day. That day, she made a promise to herself to live every day as if it were her last. Ana did what no one with a single ventricle had ever done. She got married, got pregnant, and had a child, which sent her into cardiac failure. Since then, her marriage had crumbled, and she was moving on. She had a fierce determination to fight for justice and a life well lived.

My tennis friends, the Bumblers, were there week after week, trying to make me laugh and forget my fears.

"Pam, what's the story with Fernando this week?"

"Pam, someday you will find the strength, and you'll have the kind of determination you have in the tennis courts."

"Hit him in the head with a racket so he comes to his senses."

Their words always made me laugh. I stopped playing tennis completely after I asked for the divorce, but I still went to see them play so I could be around them.

In January 2005, I told my team I was moving out. "I need to leave the house. Fernando isn't leaving, and things are only getting worse and escalating. I've saved some money over the past year from the grocery money, enough for a deposit and mattresses."

"We're here and ready for when you need us," said Helena. "We all have extra dishes and kitchen supplies. Between all of us, we also have some furniture we don't use. It's all for you to use and dispose of, as needed." Helena and I had a special bond. We had been co-captains one year. "Generosity" was her middle name.

"Have you told the kids?" asked Sylvia, whom I referred to as my happy friend. She always had a smile.

"No, I haven't told them we'll be moving out. Mr. Curry said I needed to stay in the house, but I can't any longer. I'm prepared to tell them the day we move, not before."

"I'll pick up the girls and do something with them the day you move," Sylvia said. "Let's make a plan."

I told my friends I was waiting for the right time, but talking with them all filled me with courage. Tennis was my sport. I loved being in the courts, I loved hitting the ball, and I loved the freedom I felt when I was playing. Most of the ladies' husbands were friends, but since Fernando had never cared for sports, he never did anything related to them. As I lost my Latin friends, I held on to my tennis ones.

I had angels who silently questioned why I stayed. Luz Maria with her gentleness always encouraged me to find my way. She knew I was the only one who could make the choice.

I had friends who were pushed away by Fernando, whom I didn't fight for until it was to late: Elsa, my sister in law, Maru, Gisela, Juliana, Diana, Maria, Gaby, Mildred, and many more who were once part of my life.

All of these girlfriends were my lifelines to survival. Girlfriends, who were there for births, baptisms, birthdays, illnesses, and funerals. Girlfriends, who were angels in our life.

THE MOVE
FEBRUARY 2005

One morning in February 2005, I saw Fernando leave the house with a small suitcase. He was excited and in a strange mood. He had started leaving sporadically for one or several nights. I never knew if he would be home or not when I got home. When the car left the driveway, I called my tennis friends and my mother, then proceeded to find the children. I needed to talk to them.

"Children, you know Papi is getting sicker. It's not safe at home anymore," I said with conviction. "Papi has been cleaning his rifles in the closet every night for the past two weeks after midnight. I don't know if he'll do something crazy with them. Guns and hiding don't go together. We need to leave the house. We've talked about this before, and it's time."

"Where did he go, Mami?" Natalia asked, looking at me curiously.

"He left on a trip. He just drove off to the airport. I don't know where he's going or when he's coming back. I couldn't find his passport, so I know he left. I rented a place two weeks ago, but I've been waiting for the right moment for us to leave, and I believe that's today. You can only take your clothes. I have black garbage bags to make it easier. Grandma and Anne will be here any minute. Please hurry; just grab your favorite things. We have to be out this morning. I bought mattresses, and my tennis friends are all giving us some furniture, kitchen appliances, and pots and pans."

I was excited. The time had come.

Anne, Sylvia, and my mother all arrived around nine o'clock. It was a Saturday morning.

We started working frantically, without talking. I knew Fernando had left with his bags packed, but I also knew his behavior had been erratic and he could turn right around and come back.

"Mami, I'm scared. What will Papi say when he comes home and doesn't find us here?" Christy, my oldest daughter, asked, looking at me anxiously.

"I don't know, but it's getting too dangerous to stay. Hurry up. Just put your clothes in the bag, and then I'll do the rest."

"Mami, what about the dogs, my iguana, and our guinea pigs? Can they all come with us?" Natalia asked, holding Cookie, our boxer.

Cookie had been with us for three years, and Rocky, an English cocker spaniel, had been with us for four. I knew I couldn't take them. My lease was for a house without pets. Slowly, I told Natalia, "We can take the iguana. The guinea pigs have to stay, and I think it'll be too hard for the dogs to move. They have a yard here, and we don't really have a place for them there. You'll see them when you come to visit Papi."

My heart ached as I said it. I had thought about so many things, yet I knew leaving the dogs would be hard, especially for Natalia. I held her in my arms as she cried. "I'll take care of them till Papi comes back. I've already made arrangements for that. Please, go get ready."

She dried her tears. "Mami, help me pack my clothes. I need to go find my iguana." Then she ran off to find the lizard. As we packed, Christina came over and hugged me.

"I wanted to go to boarding school to get away, but this will work. But it still hurts a lot, Mami." Tears began flowing down her face. I dropped the clothes on the floor and took her in my arms.

"I know it hurts. I'm sorry it has to be like this." We held onto that moment, time stopping for a few seconds. Eventually, we both let go and resumed our work.

Nicholas and Natalia didn't say much throughout the morning. I watched them as I helped them pack their clothes, and I hugged them. No words were necessary. They were younger, but they were aware that we were leaving their beloved home. I often remember that particular day with the children. They were strong. Maybe they were afraid to disappoint me, maybe the pain had numbed them, and maybe they had just been waiting for me to make the decision. But everyone was scrambling to gather their things.

As I looked around the house, I knew I was leaving all the things we had bought together. All the memories, all the books, and worst of all, all the pictures of our life together. I picked up the photo albums and started browsing through them. I saw pictures of our wedding, our honeymoon, the birth of our children, their first steps, the smiling faces at birthday parties, the Halloween parties—and tears filled my eyes. I had been married for sixteen years, and now I was leaving secretly while he was gone.

"Pam, you can't look at that right now," Anne said. "It will make this more difficult, and we're running out of time. Bring some if you want to."

"Anne, I can't. Mr. Curry said I needed to leave with only our clothes. I'm only supposed to take my things and the children's— nothing that is shared. Besides, it will be harder for him. He needs the memories of the family. I can't take that away. I just wanted to remember everything that was good. A marriage is a combination of both the good and the bad. I have to remember the good times also, or my life with him will not make any sense at all."

I was anxious, but I was also happy. I had woken up with newfound courage. It had taken me years to get to this day. Everything was done in secrecy and planned over months. I had saved what little money I could under my mattress. Daily, I had repeated the mantra "baby steps" and prayed for courage. I had memorized the serenity prayer when I had gone to Alcoholics Anonymous.

"God, grant me the serenity to accept the things I cannot change, the courage to change the things I can, and the wisdom to know the difference."

I had found a place I could rent for a year in Sugar Land. Throughout the morning, we went back and forth between the new place and our old home. When we were finally ready to lock the door and leave, I walked around the house. It had been home when we first moved in. As our marriage deteriorated, it had become a prison. A house is a home when love is present, but the shadow of Alcohol had lingered in the background. I was relieved to say goodbye to Alcohol and his friend Fear.

Earlier that morning, the children had called their friends and told them we were moving. When we arrived at our new place, the children's friends were all waiting to help them organize their clothes. Nicholas's best friends, Alan, Andres, and Daniel, had also brought a soccer ball.

"Nico, let's play soccer first," Alan said, bouncing the ball on his leg. "We can help you later."

Nico looked at his friends, then looked at his room, which was filled with unpacked clothes. He smiled at his friends before looking at me. "Mom, I promise we'll fix my room later. I really want to go play soccer. Is that okay with you?"

"Yes, of course," I said, smiling. "I think you need to go with your friends. You'll have time to fix the clothes later." I wanted him to be happy. He rushed outside and kicked the ball with force.

As we unpacked, there was sadness and exhaustion mixed with the emotions of a new adventure. "Natalia, this is so cool," said her best friend, Rachel, trying to cheer her up. "We can decorate your room, then we can play with your iguana. We'll make a special girls club here."

"I'm going to miss the dogs, Rachel," Natalia stated anxiously. They might forget about me."

"Natalia, a new place to live doesn't mean you won't see them again. You'll see them when your dad comes back. When people get divorced, they just go back and forth. It can be fun. Let's unpack so we can explore the neighborhood." Rachel emptied Natalia's clothes onto her new bed.

That evening around seven, after all the friends had left, we gathered in the living room. Everyone was tired after a day full of emotions and work, but we had to have a family meeting. These were always a blessing for me as a mom. They were times to share feelings openly and to clear the air of any misunderstandings. This particular time, I wanted to listen and be present, to reassure them that they were loved by Fernando and me, despite us moving on.

"Children, I ordered pizza for tonight. We can go walking later and look at the neighborhood. We'll continue to celebrate everything we can in life. I know that if we are together, we'll be okay."

"Mami, it was time, but we still love Papi." Christy had tears streaming down her pale face as she hugged Natalia. "This is difficult for all of us, but it needed to be done. I just hope it's not too hard on Papi when he gets home and can't find us."

I stared at my oldest daughter. *How can she be so wise at such a young age?* She was fourteen, but she already understood how Alcohol had come and stayed.

We ate pizza on the floor of the living room and started laughing. There was peace in the air. Fear did not accompany us that night.

"Mami, let's get a dog," Natalia said.

"Natis, let's settle in first. Besides, we're renting. Dogs aren't allowed in this house. You have an iguana; it's like a dog." I smiled, knowing the words wouldn't be enough, but hoping to convince her otherwise.

"No, not really. It's a reptile. Different species, Mami." Christy laughed.

"Mami, if we can't get a dog, then let's get a cat," Natalia argued. "We've never had a cat, and they're easy to take care of."

"A cat? Let me think about that. A cat comes with a litter box, and I don't want to be the one stuck cleaning it!"

They all looked at each other, then at me, smiling. "Mami," Nicholas said, "we'll take care of it. I've always liked cats."

Over the next couple of days, we started making the house a home. I took the children to IKEA, and we bought basic furniture. IKEA was a great place to get set up; everything was labeled *easy assembly*. At home, with boxes and instructions on how to set up drawers scattered across the floor, we all realized that easy meant different things to different people. Fortunately, my friend Anne showed up that evening with a different kind of box.

"Hey, Pam, I got a present for you. Half the problem you're having is that you don't have the right tools."

I took the box from her and opened it to find a beautiful pink toolbox filled with tools. I smiled at her as she said, "You need one. I'll teach you how to use everything. I learned from my dad when I was a child. My favorite is the drill."

I laughed. "I feel really empowered now, Anne!"

Two weeks later, assembling things had become easier.

When renting, one sometimes finds themselves in a place where everything breaks down. That was what happened to us. The first week in, the microwave went out, and our landlord decided it wasn't his responsibility to replace it. A few weeks after our move, Christina and I were in the kitchen fixing dinner when we realized the floor was flooded with soapy water. We looked at each other and started laughing nervously as we tried to walk, but we slipped and fell to the soapy floor. Christy, we realized, had turned the dishwasher on and used dish soap by mistake.

"Don't you love this?" I asked, sitting in a puddle of water. "It's life!"

"Mom, I hate it. I want to be a princess with a housekeeper. I hate it all!"

Christy started sobbing. We were both soaking wet. I moved close to her and held her until her tears dried up. There was silence as we sat on the flooded floor. I thought, *It's been hard for them, but they are my strength and my reason to go on.*

After about fifteen minutes, Christy smiled. "Mami, it's not bad. It's really better. We don't have to hide at night, and we can go on long walks in the evenings."

A few days later, we were all gathered in the living room, siting on the rug, when my cell phone started ringing. I looked at the number and then at the children, who watched my every move, not taking their eyes off me. My thoughts raced. *He's back.* My hands trembled, and my heart raced. I took deep breaths. Fear tried to embrace me, but I pushed it away as I struggled to stay calm. Slowly, I picked up the phone after several rings. "Hello?"

"Where are you? Where are the kids? Why did you leave? I'm back. You need to come back." His voice was loud, and I sensed his anger.

"We moved out two weeks ago. We can't come back. You didn't even tell me where you were going or when you'd return. You were supposed to move out so I could stay in the house with the kids, but you refused. I've already called the police twice in the last six months. I can't anymore. I need to put distance between us. I had to leave. We are causing more harm than good to each other right now."

There was a period of silence, and then I heard the words, "I will fight."

I breathed slowly, mentally counting to four to remain calm, but I was shaking.

"The kids. We need to work this out for the kids. I rented a place not far away, and I'll give you the address. You can see them. They can visit, but they sleep in the new house."

As I said this, I felt relief. I had a voice. I was speaking out as I hadn't done in years. I continue taking deep breaths as the conversation finished. Holding the phone in my hands, I calmly put it down.

"Children, Papi is back. He knows we left, and he knows you're living here. He'll see you all this weekend."

They stared at me with looks of disbelief, but slowly, they smiled. I looked at them, and then I ran to the bathroom, where I vomited uncontrollably from the stress. With time, this reaction would stop as I reclaimed my voice forever.

JOB HUNTING

In the months that followed, I looked for jobs. It was difficult. I didn't have a lot of money left. I had gone through most of my secret mattress savings. I didn't have a credit card or any credit to get one with. Fernando's child support payments came through some months, but other months, I scrambled to make ends meet. The Catholic schools the children attended were aware of the situation and helped me with payment plans until I could get back on my feet.

Sleepless night followed, and I was exhausted. I wanted to sleep all day. Mom came by every day. She was always smiling and always had the right words to say.

One day, when she found me reading job listings in the living room, she said, "You look tired. What can I do today to help you? I brought you food. I'll pick up the kids."

"I can't sleep," I replied. "I'm afraid to take sleeping pills. I'm tired all the time. Mom, do you think I'm depressed, or do you think I'm sick?" I hoped her answer would relieve my chronic fatigue.

She put the grocery bags filled with food on the floor and sat on the white sofa beside me for a while. Then she answered, calmly holding my hand. "I think you're depressed. You have been through a lot. Your body has gone into shock and is trying to recover. You'll get through this. Some things just have to be lived."

I closed my eyes and laid back on the sofa. Depression was the last thing on my mind. I had children to worry about. I prayed for help. *Jesus, I need you. Help me.*

Job hunting was stressful. I searched for work on the internet. I read ad after ad and made phone calls. I asked my girlfriends what I was good at and if they knew anyone who was hiring. I updated my resume, sending out daily applications online. I went on interviews. Then I waited.

One day, I was complaining about the bills and the cost of everything at the dinner table when Nicholas got angry.

"Mom, just get a job. I don't want to hear how expensive everything is and how we need to cut down expenses. Please, just get a job."

I stared at him in disbelief, hurt and frustrated that he didn't understand where I was coming from. "I'm trying, Nico, I'm really trying. Do you know how hard it is to find a job?"

He put down his silverware and looked me in the eye. "Mom, you have never given up on us. You have always been there. I am not giving up on you. Mom, we need you." Then he moved his chair back, came over, and gave me a long hug. I felt his concern and his love.

After a few seconds, he said, "I'm going to go play soccer. I'll see you later. The guys are waiting for me. Loved the food tonight." He ran off, bouncing the soccer ball with his knees. The conversation had drained me, but I made a choice at that moment: no more complaining about the cost of things.

I was always grateful for that round piece of polyester that held a latex rubber bladder filled with air. It brought my son joy as he kicked it around daily. The soccer ball always reminded me of his resilience. Now, I needed to be resilient.

I decided to take the first job I could find. I couldn't stay in bed and hide from the world. I needed to show my children that their mother was strong and courageous. It had been my choice to leave, and I had a responsibility to take care of them. I was determined to find a job.

Bills piled up. Pounds came and went with the stress. I continued to pray as I waited, searched for jobs, and dreamed of being hired.

One morning in April, I received a promising phone call. Natalia was walking with me when the phone rang.

"Hello. Can I help you?" I greeted, not recognizing the number.

"Is this Pamela Lombana?" asked a male voice with an eastern accent.

"Yes, it is. Who is this?" I was suspicious of the voice on the other end of the line.

"I'm Khalid. I'm the director of the Americas Refugee Clinic located in Bellaire. I saw your application and would like for you to come in for an interview."

I couldn't believe what I was hearing. Natalia's curiosity took over, and she tried to listen in on the conversation.

"Yes, when? I'm available tomorrow, if you are." I tried not to sound too excited, but I was smiling the whole time. Natalia made happy faces and clapped her hands while I was on the phone.

"Tomorrow at ten, I have an opening. We'll see you then. I assume you have the address."

"Yes, I'll be there. Thank you for calling." I put down the phone, and Natalia and I hugged each other and started jumping up and down.

"We need to go home now, Natis. I need to plan what to wear tomorrow." We walked home rapidly and straight into the closet to sort out clothes. At dinner that night, I told the children, "We need to pray for my interview tomorrow." The children were as excited as I was. The next morning, as I dropped them off at school, each one shared words of encouragement and support.

I arrived for the interview early at a tall white building. I could tell it had been there for a while: the paint was old and the lighting dim. I went up to the tenth floor, and the elevator opened onto a hallway that led to a door that read *Americas Clinic*. I knocked on the door, and a heavyset lady opened it.

"I'm hear to see Mr. Khalid. I have an interview with him."

"Are you the nurse practitioner?" she asked curiously.

"Yes, I arrived a little early," I responded, looking her in the eye.

"Just wait in the reception area. I'll tell him you're here." She smiled as she left to notify him.

I looked around as I waited. The walls were washed out and bare. The floor was covered in a dark brown carpet, and the reception area looked like it had been decorated thirty years ago. A few minutes passed before a thin man of about five and a half feet with a dark complexion approached me with a big smile. He had a kind face and dark eyes and wore glasses.

"Hello, I'm Khalid. It's good to meet you. Come to my office, and we'll talk about the position."

"Yes, of course," I said, following him to his office. "Thank you for interviewing me today. I'm really interested in this job." I wondered as I spoke where his accent was from. Khalid looked at me silently for a moment and smiled.

"Have you ever worked with refugees before?"

"Not really, but I've worked in a medically underserved clinic with the Hispanic community, so it might be similar," I said confidently.

"It's not quite the same. This is a challenging environment. Most of the patients were just released from refugee camps.

They don't know anything about life in America; everything is new to them, even electricity. The majority of the children were born in the camps. Poverty has surrounded their lives, and most come from war-torn areas. They were forced to leave or die. Everyone knows someone who was killed. They don't speak English, only their native tongues or dialects, so you'll work with a translator. We work mostly with refugees from Somalia and Sudan right now. The whole family usually comes into the clinic together; it's a family affair, so don't expect much privacy in the rooms. They are all still experiencing culture shock." He spoke calmly as he continued to explain the difficulties the clinic encountered. He smiled as he talked; he appeared to truly love his position.

"I believe I'm the right person for this position," I said once he'd finished he explanation. "My passion is helping others, and the plight of the refugees is close to my heart. What will the salary and benefits be?"

"No benefits. This is a pilot program, an incubator grant. Money is limited. If the program is successful, we'll be able to keep the grant going, and we'll consider benefits. The job is yours if you want it." He sighed. "Nobody wants to work without benefits, so we're having a hard time staffing the clinic."

The hourly pay was low for a nurse practitioner and I needed health insurance, but I had applied at so many different places already without success. "It'll be hard without benefits, but I'll take it. When do I start?"

"Tomorrow. Can you be here at eight in the morning? It's an eight-to-four schedule, and you'll have thirty minutes for lunch. I'll have the receptionist start calling the patients for tomorrow. Your medical director will be Dr. Patzakis; you'll meet him tomorrow. He usually comes once a week for several hours.

Let's get some papers signed, and I'll get everything ready for the clinic to reopen." He smiled and thanked me for taking the job.

Afterward, I left the building, went to the dollar store, and bought two dozen helium-filled balloons. I wanted to celebrate. These were baby steps, but I was slowly moving forward. That evening, my mother picked the children up from school as I wanted to keep the news a secret until they got home. When they opened the front door, I greeted them with the words, "Tonight, we celebrate. I have a job!" They jumped and screamed in joy, running to give me a group hug.

I smiled and raised my hands to heaven. "I love my life. Come on, all of us: I love my life. Together."

We all laughed and raised our hands, repeating our favorite chant. It was something I had done frequently as the kids were growing up. During bicycle rides or walks, I would raise my hands and, smiling, say in a loud voice, "Kids, I love my life. Come on, everyone together: I LOVE MY LIFE!" Slowly, the words had disappeared as I lost my voice. That day, I redis-covered them.

Weeks went by, and I loved my job. My children, my mom, and I began painting the clinic. My children's friends, Andres, Daniel, Alan, and Jose, came to help, along with Alan and Jose's uncle Ricardo, a professional painter and carpenter from Mexico. It was an old building, but we made it colorful for the patients. We painted the rooms yellow and decorated them with children's posters that we bought at Walmart.

I looked forward to seeing my patients from Somalia. They all came dressed up in bright colors, with turbans on their head and long skirts that covered their feet and their plastic sandals. It was a beautiful contrast against their shiny dark skin. When-ever I saw patients, everyone stood around the examination table. They were fascinated by the stethoscope, the ophthalmo-scope, and the otoscope. They wanted turns listening to each other's heart and looking into each other's mouth and ears. In the early days, I tried to provide privacy for each patient, but they never seemed to mind not having it.

One day, I drew blood from a three-year-old, and he just stared at me. There was no reaction. No sense that he was in pain. He didn't withdraw his arm. He didn't cry. He had old circular burn scars all over his body. I asked Fatima, the translator about it.

"The family just got here," she replied, carefully embracing him. "He was born in a refugee camp, and that was home. We know he talks, but he's still afraid. Those are cigarette burns on his skin. He was probably punished, or they believed they were curing him from an illness. He'll learn to laugh and play, but it will take time."

Another day, when I was performing a Pap smear, I found the effects of female genital mutilation in a young patient, around seventeen years old. Her vaginal area was so scarred that I couldn't proceed. I had read about it and seen pictures in nursing school, but seeing it made me sick. As I examined her, the young woman stared at the wall, tears flowing down her cheeks. I had Fatima ask her about it.

"When did this happen?" Fatima asked, holding her hand and wiping her tears.

"After I got my period, they came during the night and took me from my hut. I was afraid and screamed, but that didn't stop them from cutting me." She continued to tell her story as she sobbed in Fatima's arms.

My mother fell in love with the clinic and the children. She wanted to help them learn English faster, so she regularly showed up with children's books from the library. She would

111

spend several hours a day reading to the patients in the waiting room and the examination rooms as they waited to be seen.

One morning, she brought brightly colored fingernail polish, and the little girls couldn't stop smiling. They silently lined up, waiting their turn to have their fingernails painted. We communicated through the translator, through smiles, and through our hands.

At nights and on weekends, I wrote in my diary, and I wrote letters to Christina, Nicholas, and Natalia. I wanted to remind them of the love I had for them and how, every day, they gave me a reason to live. I wrote them letters for every special occasion in their lives and, sometimes, just to remind them how much I loved them. Being a single parent was not easy, but we had gained peace in our lives.

LAUGHTER

Months passed, and laughter filled our home. I decided to do things differently by not following any decorating rules. I wanted the children to be inspired and creative. In our first home, nothing had been allowed on the walls except oil paintings. This new start meant I could allow them to be creative.

Christina decorated her room by covering one wall in magazine pages. Natalia, my free spirit, wanted purple and green, with beads and lights all over. She had always reminded me of Ralph Waldo Emerson's words: "Do not go where the path may lead, go instead where there is no path and leave a trail." In my room, I put up posters and pictures with positive affirmations. I needed to read them daily.

My friend Anne, from Lafayette, was petite and thin, and she had been blessed with the ability to organize anything. She continued to come over to help decorate and arrange furniture. She always brought laughter into the house.

One day, she came over with a pot of gumbo, a green salad, and some white rice. I was on the floor in the living room, assembling a desk. Anne had just come from yoga class, so she was wearing sweatpants and a loose shirt.

"I knew you were going to be putting that together this morning," Anne said. "I'm here to help, and I brought food so we can sit and eat after we finish."

"Thank you," I said. "I love Cajun food."

At one point while we were assembling the desk, Anne looked up at me. "Pam, the kids are happy. I see them smiling a lot more. But how is Fernando doing?"

"He seems to be okay. Our relationship is very strained right now, and communication is minimal, except for the children. He picks them up from school on Wednesdays to take them to dinner, and he tries to see them on weekends. It's peaceful here at home. I had forgotten what it was like to live without drama in my life. I stayed because I truly believed it was the best thing for the children to have their parents together, but right now, I'm not sure it's worth doing that in situations like mine."

One day, I was home fixing dinner when Nicholas ran in excitedly.

"Mami, you won't believe what happened today," he said, eyes glowing. "A girl from eighth grade kissed me at the movies. My legs were shaking, and I couldn't walk."

"Who is this girl?" I asked, surprised. "How do you feel?"

"She's the friend of a friend. She's a year older than I am. It was really strange, Mami. Is it normal to shake like that?"

I smiled and, curious, asked, "Was this your first kiss?"

"Yes, Mami."

"It's normal. But be careful with girls. They'll make your head spin. Did I ever tell you about my first kiss?"

"No, Mami," he replied, looking curious.

"When I was at LSU, I was asked to go to a military ball by this handsome sophomore in one of my classes. After the dance, he French-kissed me. I was so shaken by the wet kiss and the tongue that I ran into my dorm and cried. So it seems you had a better experience than I did."

We both started laughing, but I knew I needed to drill the hormone talk. Hormones and how they could truly disrupt one's life if they were given free range. Hormones, which were tied to so many emotions and behaviors.

Two weeks after that, Natalia's new corn snakes got lost in the house. As I walked into the living room, I heard Christina and Nicholas shouting. They stood on the sofa, arguing with Natalia and refusing to come down.

"What is going on?" I asked, exasperated. "Why are you all fighting, and why are you on the sofa?"

"The snakes are lost," Christina and Nicholas answered loudly in unison. "They're not in their cage."

"Mami, why did you let her have snakes? We already have an iguana. None of my friends' sisters have reptiles. None of them! We're not getting off the sofa until those reptiles are found." Christina waved her hands, her expression determined.

"They're only corn snakes, and they're only twelve inches long. They can't hurt you," I replied, trying to bring some order to the chaos. "I'm also afraid of snakes, Christy, but Natalia loves them." I had decided to act cool. I could look at the snakes, but I couldn't touch them. I cringed every time I helped her feed them small pink frozen mice.

Natalia and I spent the next two hours moving furniture until we finally found them. Natalia wore a huge smile, and everyone was relieved. I wanted to get rid of the snakes, but she loved her white albinos. She loved animals in general, and our house had begun to look like a zoo. We had already acquired a cat, a gerbil, the iguana, and the corn snakes.

A month later, the gerbil fell out of his rolling ball, and the cat went after him. I came home to find Nicholas and Natalia furiously screaming at the poor cat.

"What do you think he is, food? If you get close to my gerbil, I'll put you outside," Nico screamed, chasing the cat.

"It's a predator after prey. What do you all expect?" Christina asked, lifting her head from doing homework in the breakfast room.

"It's not nice to eat somebody from the same family," Nico screamed, still trying to save the gerbil.

We all started laughing at the craziness of his comment. The gerbil was rescued by Natalia before Shadow, the cat, could make a meal of him.

As months passed, a lightness filled the air. The children and I laughed every day, especially at night. There was a special bond developing between them. In the last years, they had spent more and more time alone; the girls had immersed themselves in books, Nicholas in video games. Since we had moved out of the house, there was organized chaos, laughter, and communication flowing between everyone. There was still a schedule to be followed with school, but life was more relaxed. Living in a smaller area also allowed us to be together more often.

Seven or eight months after we had moved, Christy noticed that Nicholas had become very interested in girls. Wanting to talk, she came into the breakfast room, where I was reading a journal.

"Mami, have you noticed that Nico has girl ADD?

"You mean girl attention deficit disorder? Why do you say that?" I asked, curious and amused by her usage of the words.

"Every day, he has a different crush. It's like every time he looks a different way, he sees another girl and he likes her. Is that normal, Mami?" Her manner was so serious and her look so questioning, I felt like laughing, but I knew this was important to her if she had brought it to my attention.

"Really? I knew he got kissed; he was pretty excited about that. I think his hormones have kicked in. I better make sure I give him the sex talk. If girls become more important than soccer, though, we know he's in trouble!"

The sex/hormone talk started when they were around ten

years old, and the response was always the same: "Mami, *no . . .* gross . . . !"

That evening, our dinner conversation provided a chance to begin the topic with Nico. He had invited over his regular friends, Andres, Alan, and Daniel.

"I had a teenager at the clinic today," I said. "She's fourteen years old and pregnant."

They looked at me, faces mortified as they obviously wondered where I was going with this.

"If you have sex, use protection. Don't get a girl pregnant; you'd have to be financially responsible for the baby. And don't forget, herpes stays with you forever, and HIV kills."

"Mami . . . we have friends over. You're going to embarrass them!" Natalia said, giggling.

I smiled. "I'm saving them from child support and diaper changing."

One evening in the fall, it was getting dark outside, and we couldn't find Natalia. We had all been watching TV when I first noticed she was gone.

"Nico, Christy, where's Natis? I haven't seen her in a while."

"Mom, she went to pick flowers in the neighborhood," Christina stated.

"It's been a long time. Let's go find her. She's making me nervous. I don't want her to get kidnapped."

Nico laughed. "Mami, we live in the States. That only happens in Colombia."

I knew he was right, but I also knew I wouldn't be at peace until we found her.

A few minutes later, we'd all walked outside to go search for Natalia when we saw her walking down the sidewalk toward the house, her hands full of wildflowers. We all looked at each other with relief.

Natalia and I started an herb garden, though it didn't prosper. She had also started growing green, yellow, and brown fungi in petri dishes in her room. She was always doing different experiments, and I encouraged her, thinking she might be a scientist someday.

At home, Nicholas always had a soccer ball in his hand and was continually bouncing the ball in the air and kicking it up with his heels and his knees.

"Nico, go play outside," I'd say sternly. "You're going to break a window."

"Mami, I'm too good to break a window. I'm a great soccer player." He'd smile at me as he walked out the door, the soccer ball in his hands.

One day, he was bouncing the ball in the entrance of the house when I heard glass shatter.

"Nicholas, what have you done?" I screamed, already knowing the answer.

"Mami, the ball just went there, through the glass door. I don't know how it happened. I'm sorry, Mami. I'll pay for it." He wore an expression of disbelief as he stared at the glass-strewn floor.

"Nico, we don't have any extra money, and this is expensive." I stared at him in frustration, then looked at all the glass on the floor.

"Mami, I'll do chores to repair the door. I'll start working. I'm really sorry." He met my eyes with a look of guilt, the soccer ball still in his hands.

"Make him wash everybody's clothes," screamed Natalia from another room. She hated washing clothes. "He's really good at that." She came into the foyer then to see what the commotion was about.

"That sounds like a great idea," I said. "Nico, what do you

think? For the next month, you'll have to wash and fold everybody's clothes."

"Okay, Mami. That's a deal. I'm really sorry, Mami. I'll pay you back. I promise never to play inside again."

"You'll pay for it by working. There are consequences to your actions in life, so think before you do things."

Nicholas washed and folded clothes for six months. His sisters never said a word when the first month ended. Finally, he came to me one evening when I was reading in my bedroom.

"Mami, how long was I supposed to do all the laundry?"

I smiled. "One month."

"So why am I doing everyone's laundry?"

"Well, the girls hate doing it, and you are really good at it. You never said anything when the month was up, so neither did they. Just tell them they need to wash their own clothes now."

Time continued to heal us all. I loved planning special events and getting the children together with their friends. As our second Valentine's Day on our own approached, I didn't have a date, so I started a new family tradition.

"Christy, Nico, Natalia, let's celebrate Valentine's Day together with a real party."

"Like a party with our dates, but with friends?" Christy asked.

"Yes, a real dinner party," I responded.

"Mami, we can have everyone dress up and make it a fancy affair," Christy stated happily.

"We can decorate the table and make it special," Natalia said, her eyes shining with anticipation. "Can we have chocolate? Oh, I love parties!"

"My friends love your parties, Mami. They'll all come," said Nico.

Valentine's Day—a day cherished or hated, a day that can bring out feelings of loneliness or happiness—became one of our greatest celebrations. Year after year, we decorated the house with balloons and the tables with red cloths and chocolates. I prepared elegant sit-down dinners. Everyone invited came dressed up, talked, laughed, ate, and left with a special bag of candy.

Life had settled in. The children saw their dad weekly, but they were always happy to be back home. However, they really loved it when he took them out to eat with their friends. I cooked meals at home most of the time. Eating out was a luxury.

LETTER TO MY CHILDREN
NOVEMBER 26, 2005

Dear Christina, Nicholas, and Natalia,

I didn't want this weekend to pass without telling you how much you all mean to me. Life has a way of giving, taking, and constantly changing. I am thankful for the time life has given me with you. You have been my reason to live, to laugh, to work, to dream, and to go on.

Some decisions in our lives have not been easy, and some changes in your lives have been difficult. I admire your courage and your strength under the circumstances. You've taught me how to laugh when all I wanted to do was cry. You gave me hugs and smiles during times of trial.

I've tried to do my best as a parent. Someday, you may only remember the chauffeur, the cook, the massages I gave you, and the errands we all ran, but I pray that you remember all the love I've had for you and all the laughs we've had together!

Mami

DIVORCE

On December 29, 2005, I arrived at the courthouse an hour ahead of schedule. This was the day I would sign my divorce papers. I sat in the car in the parking lot and stared at the old red-brick building. I wondered how many lives had been changed in this building. I had come several years earlier to be present at an adoption that had taken place in the family court. That had been a happy time for Judy, a friend of mine from tennis.

This day, however, I was alone. Anne had offered to come, but I told her I needed to take this final step by myself. Finally, I exited the car, went up the stairs, and opened the door to the building. It had a musty smell and stark white walls. Finding the elevator, I took it to the floor of the building I had been assigned to.

Most doors on the floor were closed as the courts were in session. However, Mr. Curry had also arrived early and was waiting for me. When I saw him, I smiled. I hadn't eaten or slept much in the last twenty-four hours. My head throbbed, my hands were sweaty, and my heart beat heavily. When he looked at me, I knew he could see I was tired. We sat in silence for a while.

"Are you ready?" he finally asked. "It's been thirteen months since I first met you in my office. It'll be okay. This is the easy part. It will be okay, and he will also be okay. We have done it correctly. You both have custody, and you both love the kids. You continue to do the best you can as a single parent. It's not an easy road, but you love, encourage, and support them. Just enjoy them a day at a time." There was a serenity in his face as he spoke.

"Thank you for helping me," I replied, tears in my eyes. "I thought I'd be celebrating and rejoicing today, but I feel only sadness in my heart."

"Whenever there has been great love, there will always be pain. Just don't ever forget that he has an illness; you need to remember that. I'm old enough to have seen your story many times. I want you to start taking care of yourself. Someday, you'll want to start dating again."

"I'm not sure about that, Mr. Curry. How will I know when I'm ready? I'm still afraid."

"Someday, you'll be happy and excited when someone asks you out. Life doesn't stop with a divorce. You have to live your life, or it will pass you by. Someday, you might even want to get married again; time heals, if you allow it. You'll learn to embrace each new day."

"Mr. Curry, someday we'll go out and celebrate. And if I ever get married again, you'll be first on the wedding list." We both laughed.

Mr. Curry was an older man, probably in his mid-seventies. He was a man of integrity. The first time I had gone to see him, I couldn't stop crying. I had been in a state of panic. He listened and guided me, and over that year, he became my friend and mentor. At first, he'd worked with both Fernando and me, but eventually it was only with me. He tried to make it right for both of us. He had lived long enough to see the destruction and pain caused by divorce. He knew that only time could heal the wounds.

We would stay in touch over the next few years. Mr. Curry always asked about Fernando and the children. He always had great advice. He died several years after the divorce was finalized. I went to visit him at the hospital several days before his death. I just sat, held his hand, and thanked him for being in my life.

I've been asked throughout my life if my divorce was fair.

Divorce is never fair.

There is too much anger and pain involved in divorce. My divorce gave me life again and separated me from a life of fear. Economically, I lost everything, but I gained freedom. It brought me to my knees, and I searched to understand God's will in my life. Emotionally, it allowed me to start healing. I had the children with me and a reason to live.

Fernando was left alone except for his visits with the children on Wednesday evenings and every other weekend. Those weekends, the children would visit with him during the day, but at night, they would call me to pick them up. Girlfriends still came and went in Fernando's life, alcohol still lingered, but nothing could fill the void he felt.

THE MOVE
FEBRUARY 2006

Once my divorce papers were signed, I knew it was time for us to move into the city. It felt right to leave Sugar Land, and this time I was ready. I started looking for places inside the I-610 loop, closer to my job and closer to the children's schools.

One day, I walked into an older townhome complex close to Richmond and Weslayan. It was hidden by large magnolia trees and surrounded by older homes that were being purchased to be torn down. It was a quiet neighborhood in the middle of vibrant Houston.

The townhome I looked at was two stories and had three bedrooms, as well as a small open study. It was perfect for us. Each child would get their own room, I could arrange the small study to make it my bedroom. Rent and utilities were all included too. It was smaller than our last home and didn't have a yard or a garage, but it had character.

That evening, I shared the news with the children. To my surprise, they embraced it.

"I found a new place. We'll be moving into the city. It's a little smaller than this place, so we'll need to downsize again. However, rent will be more affordable, and you'll all be closer to your schools. It's an apartment complex, and it's within walking distance of the movies."

"Mami, that is going to be so much fun," Christy said, excited. "Living in the suburbs, we have to drive everywhere."

I agreed. "I think everyone should be able to pack their rooms. I'll pack the kitchen, and then we should be ready."

"That's easy, Mami," Natalia said. "We're going to be experts at packing."

"Perfect, we'll move in two weeks. Christy and Nico, start picking up as many boxes as you can from grocery stores. When you see empty boxes, just grab them."

The Saturday before we moved, I got together with my tennis friends Helena and Sylvia. We met for lunch at the La Madeleine in Sugar Land. When I arrived, they already had a table picked out. Helena was smiling and eagerly got up to meet me when she saw me.

"Pam, let's order lunch. I have some good news about spring break!"

We ordered our food and went back to the table. Immediately, Helena burst out with the news, smiling widely.

"Pam, come skiing with us. It'll be good for you and the kids. I rented a house, and I have an extra room for you and the kids. And if you want to, you can pitch in for the food."

"I'll drive my SUV, so all the kids can fit," Sylvia added, laughing. "You don't even have to buy air tickets. You can't refuse your two girlfriends."

"I'll ask the kids," I answered, excited about going on a vacation. "They all already have ski clothes, and they would love this!"

When I got home that day, I sat the children down at the dinner table.

"Helena has invited us to go skiing with her family, and Sylvia has offered to drive us up in her SUV. Do you all want to go?"

Screaming and laughter answered me.

"Heck yes, Mami!" Nicholas said. "We love skiing, and it would be fun with everyone else. Will there be any girls going?"

126

"Wait! Wait a minute," Christina interrupted. "We need to know if Mami can afford this first."

"They are inviting us," I answered, smiling. "I'll purchase the lift tickets, and we'll eat at home every day. It sounds like something we can afford."

Sylvia drove her SUV, packed full with the five of us. I slept most of the drive up and back. We spent three days skiing and laughing. I will always remember the laughter.

The day of the move came quickly, and it was a total disaster! The children had asked if they could have a sleepover party to help them pack and move. I agreed without thinking of the consequences. Ten teenagers stayed up all night, eating pizza and watching movies. Nobody wanted to get up early.

And the movers arrived at eight o'clock sharp!

"Wake up, wake up! The movers are here."

"Mami, were tired," Nicholas responded sleepily. "Give us five more minutes."

"I agreed to this party on the condition that you all would wake up and have things ready. Get up," I said, exasperated.

"Okay, Mami, we'll get up." The responses were sleepy, but they did rise.

It took all day to move. Nothing had truly been packed. On the surface, it might have seemed like we were ready, but we weren't. When we had moved out the year before, we had only taken our clothes. In the year since, we had set up a home with furniture and a lot of kitchen gadgets. We had also bought a lot of things from garage sales to decorate. I had never realized how much stuff we had accumulated until that day.

Moving into the city after living in the suburbs all our lives was like moving to a different country. The place I had found for us to live in was an old complex of small townhomes. The new place was smaller, so we had to downsize.

When the children were young, they had taken piano lessons. Nicholas had truly enjoyed the lessons and was very talented, so we purchased a baby grand piano. When I left Fernando, we took only black garbage bags filled with clothes. In the following weeks, Fernando had the baby grand we owned delivered to my new place, hoping the children would continue playing it.

As time passed, the children moved on to other things, as children often do. The piano had moved with us into the first house I'd rented, but when we moved in February 2006, I realized I had to let it go. It was the last material object I had from my life with Fernando.

The day I sold it, I said a prayer of gratitude for the music that had flowed when little hands played the keys. Music has always brought healing to my soul. The piano was the instrument my mother played and loved. I cherish memories of standing beside her as she played Mozart on her standup black piano in Colombia.

We lived in Las Palmas, the townhome complex, for two magnificent years. Everyone was part of each other's life, though we were constantly in each other's way. With four people and only two bathrooms, the mornings were chaotic.

Every morning, I woke up at five o'clock, drank coffee, and prayed in the silence of the house. At six, I started waking everyone up with coffee in bed.

"Christy, Natalia, it's time to get up. Coffee is ready. I have to wake up Nico."

"Okay, Mami. We love you, Mami," Christy or Natis would say. Then I would do the same in Nico's room.

"Nico, it's time to get up. Here's coffee."

At 6:15 a.m., I would speak more hesitantly. "Come on, kids, you need to get up. We have two bathrooms, and you need to share. You're going to be late."

128

By 6:30 a.m., chaos would break out. "Who has my vest?" Christy would ask, exasperated. "I have school mass today. Where are my socks? I can't find my white socks. Natalia, did you use my socks. I just washed clothes yesterday."

"Maybe, but I thought those were mine," Natalia would answer nonchalantly.

I would hurry to her rescue. It was hard being the youngest. "Christy, I have extra," I'd say. Or "I found some socks. Hurry, you'll be late."

Every night as the lights went off, I would say from my bedroom, "Good night. I love you, Christy, Nico, Natis. I love you."

Then everyone would answer, one by one. "Good night. Love you, Mami. Love everyone." We continued this tradition until they all left the house.

Christina and Nicholas both loved sports, and they always signed up for everything they could. Natalia, on the other hand, was never interested in them, but I felt it was important for her health. That school year, I convinced her to sign up for both soccer and basketball. After several weeks, I approached her after practice one day.

"Natalia, don't you love soccer? It's great exercise, and you're outside running."

"Mami, I hate it. I don't like sweating and smelling like grass. And the coach is mean; he thinks he can get people running by screaming at them. I'd rather be reading." By the time she fell silent, she had tears in her eyes.

"Is it that bad?" I asked, feeling guilty. I thought of the screaming she experienced when we lived with Fernando, and I knew she was only participating in sports for me, not because she wanted to.

"It is, Mami. I hate it. I hate the way he screams at us. He scares me."

Silence fell between us, and my heart hurt. I hadn't been fair to her; I needed to let her find her own path to health. I wanted her to exercise, but not under those circumstances. Looking at her, I realized I needed to respect her choices.

I hugged her. "Then I will talk to him, and you don't have to go back."

Years later, she would find her way into yoga.

CLOSING OF AMERICAS
SUMMER 2006

"Pam, we need to talk. The incubator grant was not renewed," said my boss.

"What does that mean?" I asked, holding my breath. "What happened? I thought we were growing. We have more patients; we've hired more medical assistants. What went wrong? You told me last week that you were thinking of expanding."

"It's a grant, Pam. Sometimes things fail and the money stops coming. I already have another job offer. You need to look for another job too. I'll write you a good recommendation. We only have money for one more week of payroll." As he said this, he lowered his gaze, avoiding eye contact.

He can't look me directly in the eye. He knows I'm a single parent, and he knows the struggles I go through. What about the bills? So many bills, and I have no credit. I need to act fast.

"You have one week of salary for everyone? Then you should pay us for next week and let everyone go find a job. It's the right thing to do, Khalid. We've all worked here without benefits. Give everyone a chance to stand up before they fall flat on their faces." I spoke emphatically, looking him in the eye. I was speaking with a voice that was being heard.

He looked at me, and I knew he was thinking. It didn't matter to him anymore; he already had a job offer. But he was human and had heard my request. Finally, he smiled.

"Thank you. We'll do that, but I need you to come with me to break the news. Today is the last day of Americas Refugee Clinic."

I was sick to my stomach. I had just lost my job. I had severance pay of one week. No patients had been scheduled yet, and none would be. I approached the staff, and Khalid and I told them the news. There were tears of anguish and distress, a lot of embracing and sadness as we all knew it would be the last time we'd work together or see each other. Afterward, I drove home, printed my resume and drove from clinic to clinic to submit it.

Life changes unexpectedly. When we are forced out of our comfort zone, we have to keep believing that other doors will open. That life continues.

That evening, when we were all at home, the kids asked, "Hey, Mami, can we order pizza today?"

"We need to talk," I replied. "We have to cut down on expenses again. The clinic is closing. I'm so sorry, guys, but I'm out of a job again."

Silence filled the room. We all looked at each other and then hugged. No tears were shed. They all knew Mami would get a job; it was just a question of time.

"Mami, I'll cook tonight," Christy said. "You've had a hard day. Nico, you clean the dishes. Natis, you set the table and pick a movie."

I got a job offer in less than a week, and I started working a lot. Mornings were still my quiet meditation time.

The days are long, and they want me to work weekends. I miss the time I have with the children. I miss being off when they get out. Is my life all about work now? I've become consumed by it, and when I'm home, I'm too tired to be a mom. I need a change. God, give me courage, give me guidance.

Christine, one of the nurse practitioner students I had been in charge of at the refugee clinic, approached me one day. She wanted us to find a place to work together. We soon found a clinic for sale off I-10 East. The owners were two men who were interested in reopening the clinic again. We met for dinner at a Thai restaurant to discuss arrangements. Soon after we ordered, they started calling us Charlie's Angels.

"We're going to get along great, Charlie's Angels," one of them said, smiling.

My face flushed with anger. "We have names; we're not Charlie's Angels. If we're going to continue this conversation, we need to get this clear."

"We're sorry; we didn't mean any offense. We're just happy to be able to reopen the clinic. We have a doctor who can be your medical director and sign the prescriptions for the pain management and immigration forms. We'll all be partners." He laughed confidently.

I felt a hot rush of blood go through my body, and I looked at Christine. "I need to use the restroom; I'll be back." I stood up, grabbed my purse, and pushed the chair in. Christine followed me.

"I don't like it, Christine. It's creepy, and it doesn't sound legal. I refuse to work with anyone who calls us Charlie's Angels. It's demeaning. I'll never do pain management; I don't want to lose my license, and it's not what I want to do."

"Pam, it's an opportunity to own our own clinic. Once we start, we can make our own decisions," she said, trying to convince me.

"It never works like that. If you sign up with them, it's their rules, not yours. I'm leaving. I have three children who depend on me. I can't waste time on this." I was amazed she was even considering this deal.

"Pam, if you walk out on this, I'm not including you."

"Christine, I can't. Please let them know I'm not in."

I walked away, never returning to the table. I thought of my mom and how hard she had worked. The long hours, the weekends, the fatigue. I understood her challenges. I said a prayer of gratitude for the mother I had been given, and I asked forgiveness for all my failings as a daughter.

In the next month, I got a call from an old family friend.

"Pam, this is Dr. Toro. I have a medical conference coming up, and I'll be out of the office for a week. I have coverage for the adults, but I'd like to see if you could cover me for a week with the pediatric patients."

I thought about it for only seconds before deciding to say yes. Dr. Toro and his wife, Lili, had always kept in touch with me and the children and had frequently invited us to their home.

"I'll do it," I replied excitedly. "I'll need to take time off where I'm working to help you out. It will be a different pace than what I'm doing there."

The week I covered for him, I fell in love with his practice. The patients were grateful and nice and always spoke kindly about their doctor. They saw Dr. Toro as a compassionate man. He was a man of integrity, always trying to help them, always being honest with them.

He never ordered unnecessary tests. He once told me, "When you work with cash patients, remember that they need to feed their families first. Don't order tests they don't need to enhance your income. Be an honest provider."

Two weeks after Dr. Toro returned from his conference, he offered me a full-time job. He wanted to grow his pediatric practice. It was a nine-to-five job, and I would get to go home early every day and attend my son's soccer games in the evenings. Dr. Toro did open his office for half a day on Saturdays, but he would never ask me to work that day. I happily accepted and turned in my resignation at the other clinic. I started spending more time with my children again. Life was getting better.

SUNDAY
SEPTEMBER 17, 2006

I thank God every day for my kids. I pray that they will be safe, that they will make the right choices in life. I pray that they will be strong when faced with alcohol and drugs. I pray they will be surrounded by good friends and adults in their lives. If as parents we could protect them, we would give our lives for their safety. In life, everyone has their own struggles to fight and their own battles to win. I hope I can give my children the tools to do this.

LETTER TO MY CHILDREN

Dear children,

Some people will always see the glass as half-empty. I hope you all learn to see the glass as full. I hope, my beautiful young people, that you will learn to see life as it is. Not as an easy ride, but as a great ride with ups and downs — with a combination of all the emotions. We are put on this earth to embrace life. We are here to stand up every time we fall. To walk the extra mile, to be grateful, to love, and to pray.

Love you all,

Mami

EVICTED
JANUARY 2007

One evening in January, Natalia and I had just returned from the movies and picked up the mail before going into the apartment. We were laughing and talking about the movie we had seen. I put the mail on the table and started sorting it, throwing away advertisements as I went. When I came across a letter, I didn't think much of it until I opened it.

It was a notice of eviction from the management of the apartments.

"Natalia, this is weird. It's an eviction notice." I looked at her, the paper clutched in my hands. She stood beside me, dressed in leggings, tennis shoes, and a long white T-shirt. Her young face showed confusion and disbelief.

"An eviction letter? I thought that only happened in the movies. We haven't done anything wrong, Mami. Don't worry about it. It's got to be a mistake. I told Zoe I'd help her make brownies, so I need to go." She ran up the stairs to change.

I set the letter on the table, but I was troubled. I didn't want to move again. It was after five in the evening, so I waited until the next morning to address. It was a restless night, though. The next day, I called work and told them I needed to come in two hours late, that I had a personal issue I needed to solve ASAP.

It was a cold day. A cold front had moved in overnight, and it was a brisk walk to the management office. They were going through renovations, and the office had just been painted a light gray. An older gray-haired lady with thick, heavy glasses looked up from her mahogany desk and then kept on typing on the computer. She had never been friendly, and she seemed tired of all the tenants who came in regularly with complaints.

"Hi, I'm Pam. I live at 1318 Las Palmas. I got an eviction notice yesterday. I believe there's been a mistake, so I came over to talk to you about it. I pay rent on time every month."

I handed her the letter. She took it, set it on the desk, and remained silent for a while. She stopped typing and looked up. Her face was stern, cold, and fatigued. I could tell she dreaded her job.

"I can't help you. It's the rules of the townhome association. Your son plays soccer in the streets at night with his friends, and it's disruptive to the other residents. People here complain about everything." She said the words without even cracking a smile.

"No one has ever said anything or brought this to my attention before. How can this be?"

She sighed and got up to get a folder from the file cabinet. "The security guard sees him with his friends, playing soccer in the parking lot when it's dark. We don't allow that in the town-home complex, so you have to move out. If you have questions, read the bylaws of this place. There's nothing I can do. I'm sorry."

I took the folder from her and looked her in the eye. "Can people be evicted without any previous notice?"

"If it's written in the lease agreement, yes. Anything that is disruptive to the other residents can get you evicted," she answered.

I could get an attorney, I thought, looking at her. *But that's expensive, and I don't know one. Maybe this is a blessing in disguise.* I looked at my watch and realized I needed to get to work.

I addressed her again. "I need some time to find a place, and the children are in school."

"You have a month. But you need to move out, or there will be consequences. I'm sorry about the situation, but the rules come from management." She finished in a softer voice.

I realized she was just following orders and probably hated this conversation as much as I did. I said goodbye. As I walked through the door, leaving her office, I thought, *I love this place. I don't want to move again, but if I do, it will be to someplace that no one can force me to leave. I am going to look for a place to buy. A place where no one can evict us. I'll talk to the kids tonight.*

Family meetings were a routine event, especially if big decisions had to be made. That evening, I decided to fix *ajiaco*, a delicious potato-and-chicken soup that we add capers, corn, and avocado to before serving.

When we all sat down at the table, Nicholas smiled. "What are we celebrating, Mami? You only make *ajiaco* for special occasions."

I laughed. "Christy, Nico, Natis, I know we all love this place, but we have to move. We got an eviction notice due to playing soccer at night in the parking lot."

The girls turned and looked at Nicholas, surprised. He was suddenly quiet, looking mortified.

"Nicholas, I had no idea this was a rule, so I'm not blaming you." I looked at all the children. "It's time for us to move. We need to find a new place, but I want to find a home we can buy."

"Mami, a real house?" Natalia asked. "With a yard? Can we have dogs again?" She lifted her spoon to enjoy her soup.

"Yes, a real house that will be ours. We need to look at town-homes also. Many don't have yards, but we can look. We'll start house hunting in the evenings and on weekends. Everyone has to go; this is a family affair. We'll start tomorrow. We have a month to find a place." I smiled at all of them. They smiled and laughed.

"Mom, we'll do this together," Christina said. "It will be fun, and then no one can complain. I love looking at houses. Everybody, let's eat fast so we can start looking online for a house!"

The next day after school, the search began, and everyone had an opinion.

"Mami, this one is too dark."

"Mami, this is so far from all our friends."

"Mami, it smells bad."

"I like this one, but two bathrooms is not enough for all of us."

"As long as we don't have to move into the suburbs, we'll be okay, Mami."

House hunting continued every weekend and weeknights. On the second Saturday of the month, we walked into a townhome that had been on the market for six months. It was in the Rice Military area: on Venice Street, close to Memorial Park. It was close to St. Thomas High School, which Nicholas attended, so he was excited.

"Mami, this is beautiful and open," Christina said. "It's close to our schools, and we can each have a bedroom."

"I'll take the bedroom downstairs," Nicholas said with a smile. "I've already picked it."

"I'll start looking for a dog," Natalia announced.

"No, you won't," Christina argued. "I'm the oldest. If we get a dog, I get to pick it."

"I don't think we can get two dogs right now," I said, trying to diffuse the conversation. "Let's start with one, but it has to be small. We really don't have a yard."

"Can I play with it and help with it?" asked Natalia.

"Yes, you have to help with it. And I already have a dog picked out," Christy said triumphantly. "I want a yorkipoo, and I've saved my money to buy one."

Natalia smiled at me. "Mami, you've always told us you'd love to live in Italy. The street name is Venice, so this is a sign! We can walk to Memorial Park, and we can walk to restaurants."

I looked at all my children and smiled. "It's an 'I love my life' moment. Hands in the air, together. I love my life!"

The apartment complex allowed us to extend our stay until we could get the mortgage loan and documents ready to sign and close. The three-story townhome on Venice Street had a garage and bedroom on the first floor. That one became Nicholas's room and the St. Thomas boys' hangout. It became normal for me to come home after work to find eight teenagers all sitting on the bed playing PlayStation or hear them screaming "Gooooal!" during soccer games.

The second floor became our entertainment area. It had an open floor plan, with a kitchen, dining room, and living room. It was surrounded by big open windows, so it always had light. There, we celebrated many happy moments.

The third floor was the girls' space. No males were allowed. It was estrogen city. This was the floor where dresses were tried on and discarded until the perfect one was selected, where tears were shed, and where laughter and giggling were heard. Secrets were shared on the third floor.

At that time, a physical home wasn't the only one I was looking for. I was searching for meaning in my life. My prayer life had run dry, and I had experienced rejection and anger. During this period of my life, I read books on spirituality and was always drawn to meditation. Slowly, those negative feelings were replaced with peace, gratitude, and happiness.

I missed sitting in a chapel and enjoying the silence and sanctity of holy places. Once we moved into this new townhome, I looked for a church close by.

One day, we walked into St. Theresa's at Memorial Park. At the back of the church was a huge sign on the dark paneled wall that read All Are Welcome. I knew it was an invitation to return to the church I loved and the prayers I grew up with as a child. That's also when we met Father Phil Lloyd.

From that day on, I returned weekly for mass and would line the children up after mass every Sunday to greet Father Phil.

"Mami, why do we always have to line up and greet the priest? He already knows us all," objected Nicholas one Sunday, exasperated.

"Everybody needs to know a priest, a doctor, and a lawyer. Remember that," I said, laughing, as we approached Father Phil. "Father Phil, you remember Christy, Nico, and Natalia?"

"Hello, of course I remember. Duchesne and St. Thomas. I hope you all have a great week, and God bless you all." These were the words he spoke to us, Sunday after Sunday. Slowly, the children started going to him and greeting him alone.

Sundays were family days. We went to brunch, and we planned activities. We rode bikes, we cooked, we saw movies. They knew that on Fridays and Saturdays, they could do things with friends, but Sundays were sacred for the family.

About a month after we moved in, Christina shared some exciting news at dinner. "I found a dog. It's a yorkipoo, and I negotiated for it to be flown to Houston. It's a little girl, and she'll be flying in on Wednesday. We need to go to the airport to pick her up. She'll be called Gorda."

"I'm in," said Natis excitedly.

"Sounds like a plan. Why didn't you buy a dog from Houston, though?" I asked, curious.

"Mami, people research and buy animals through the internet. It's done all the time. And by the way, everyone needs to read the book on dog training so we can all use the same techniques." Christy said this emphatically as she met each of our gazes.

142

Natalia and I made eye contact and exchanged glances. We knew we'd have to follow the rules, at least while Christy was in the house.

Gorda was Christy's dog, and every moment Christy was home, Gorda was by her side. One evening, Christina arrived home to find my mother sitting with Gorda on her lap.

"Grandma, what are you doing with that brush?"

"Oh, I borrowed it from your bathroom," my mom responded happily. "I'm just brushing my hair and brushing hers too."

"Grandma, you're brushing the dog with my brush," Christina said, looking at her grandmother with disgust.

"Oh, that's okay, Christy. We both have gray hair. Nobody will be able to tell if it's my hair or the dog's."

"Grandma, that's gross," Christina said loudly. She ran to the kitchen, where I was cooking, and stood in front of me with her hands on her hips.

"Mami, Grandma is using my brush on Gorda."

I smiled. "Christy, just hide your brushes so Mom can't find them." This became a common occurrence when my mom visited.

One day, six months after Gorda had arrived at the house, Christy was gone for the day with some friends. I opened the garage door to leave, and Gorda ran outside, out into the middle of the street. I heard the screech of car tires and a yelp of pain. I rushed to the curb as the car rapidly accelerated away. Gorda lay motionless in the street.

I was in shock as I realized what had happened. Nicholas and Natalia came running out. When they saw Gorda, they started crying. I picked up her tiny body and wrapped it in my arms. As I held her, I thought of all the love Christina had poured into this tiny creature.

I looked at Nicholas. "Nico, go bring me a towel. I need to wrap Gorda up. Christy needs to hold her and see her. In hospitals, mothers are given the opportunity to hold their deceased infants or children to help with closure."

"Mami, where are we going to put her?" Nicholas asked, tears in his eyes.

"In the freezer," I said slowly, "until Christy comes home, then we'll bury her."

He looked at me curiously and then got a towel. I gently wrapped Gorda up, making sure the untouched part of her face was visible, and put her in the freezer. When Christy came home that evening, I sat her down in the living room before she could notice that her puppy was not beside her. I gave her the news and held her while she cried. Then I brought out Gorda.

"Mami, she's frozen, hard, and cold," she cried.

"Yes, I know, but it's the only way you can truly have closure," I said.

"Mom, I know she's dead, but holding a frozen dog is creepy." She cried and gave Gorda back to me.

"I'm sorry, Christy. I know you loved her," I said softly.

That was a sad day in our life. A dog fills a home with love. We all missed having Gorda around, but Christy wouldn't hear of getting another dog. That summer, while Christina was away for two weeks, Natalia started researching small dogs on the internet. She found Sofia, a four-pound baby Italian greyhound, whom she bought with her babysitting money. With time, Christina learned to love her.

DATING

Nervousness and excitement are present in dating at all ages of life. In our early twenties, perhaps, it's filled with more anticipation than at any other time in our lives. The more experiences we live through, the more cautious we become, especially when it comes to dating and going out again.

The first person I dated after leaving Fernando turned out to be very similar to him.

I met him while I was still married. He was always nice, complimenting me and slowly saying things like "I'm sorry he doesn't see you. He's enthralled with the blonde." As time went by, his comments grew more intimate: "You look beautiful today. Someday, we will dance together."

Slowly, I was drawn into his world. Eventually, he would lay his hands on top of mine or run his hand along my arm. I thought he was being tender and supportive. Instead, I was misreading the clues.

Once I'd separated from Fernando, he started coming around the house. He made an effort to appeal to the kids, and he began to take control of my time. He became jealous and possessive. I started feeling the old, familiar fear. What had started as a comfort and reassurance of my femininity became another nightmare. It took me months to realize I was back to square one.

One evening, exasperated, Natalia told me, "Mami, what are you doing? He's just like Papi. I don't like him. I don't like him at all. Can you please talk to his ex-wife and ask her why she left him? I promise you, it's not the same story he's telling you." By the end, she was screaming and crying.

Deep inside, I knew she was right, and it shook me. It was a cold truth from the mouth of a twelve-year-old.

Why? Why did I allow him into my life? I didn't have all the answers; loneliness was one of them, but what else? I decided not to see him again, and in those last days of dating, I saw his true colors and had to get a restraining order.

I pulled back into myself for six months. Then I met someone from Argentina. I needed to trade in my car; it was too old and had too many miles on it. My friend convinced me that it would be worth it to buy a BMW. I couldn't afford a new one, so I visited a used car dealership. The man from Argentina worked there, and he helped me finalize the sale. When I got home, I was so happy I called him.

"I just wanted to call and thank you for helping me pick out this car. The children love it," I told him happily, still sitting in the car.

"Wow. I've never had anyone call me this fast to thank me for a purchase. If you have any questions about the car, just reach out to me." He paused. "Do you like the opera?"

Surprised, I answered, "Some of them. Why?"

"I have season tickets. *Carmen* will be showing next weekend. Would you like to go?"

I sat for a moment, unsure if I really wanted to go out on a date with a man. Then I took a deep breath and thought, *I need to not be afraid.*

"I'd love to go. That's one of my favorite operas."

"Great. I'll call you next week to coordinate."

It felt good. He made me laugh on our first few of dates. At first, I didn't want the children to meet him, but their curiosity was too strong. When Natalia finally met him, her expression became guarded. I could tell she didn't really like him, but I assumed it was just difficult for her to see me with someone else. She didn't say much until several months later.

"Mami, I don't like him," she said one evening as we watched TV together in the living room.

I smiled reassuringly. "Natis, we're just dating. It's not like I'm not going to marry him."

She met my eyes. "But why go out with him, then? You and I have fun together."

"I know we do, but sometimes, it's just nice to have a date," I said, not sure she truly understood.

I continued to date him for a time, but slowly I began to see what Natalia saw. I realized his lifestyle was too different from mine. He had different priorities. His mindset was "You and I are a couple; the children will grow up, and we, as a couple, come before them."

I finally broke it off, but I am still grateful for the laughter he brought into my life during that time. Through him, I met one of my current best friends, Silvia Amsel.

Natis was like a hawk; she could spot problems faster than I could. I was slower to recognize issues that affected us. As I continued moving forward in my life, I was grateful for her insight.

Fernando continued to see the children weekly. He would pick them up from school on Wednesday evenings and take them to dinner. Sometimes, they had wonderful conversations filled with laughter; other times, the children would call me to come pick them up from school because he had forgotten they had a date or he had shown up drunk. They learned to deal with the disappointments. They still tried to see him every other weekend, but those times had also lessened due to their growing interests and participation in other activities.

In the two years since I had left the house, I rarely saw him. The children would mention to me if he was using a cane or a walker, if he was eating or vomiting. Over time, they gave me descriptions of his health from every time they saw him. I silently listened. I knew his lifestyle had taken a toll on his body and health that would eventually kill him. The thought always saddened me.

FRIENDSHIPS

Silvia was Mexican and married to Sergio Amsel, who was from Argentina. They became our family when we were isolated from mine. They filled a void in our heart. The Amsels were Jewish, and they invited us to all their celebrations.

When their daughter Tammy celebrated her bat mitzvah, we were invited. We had never been to an event like it before, and we loved it. We were all excited about the invitation. For Nicholas, it was an awakening; he was surrounded by girls for the whole night.

On the way home that night, he said, "Mom, this was the best day of my life. Did you see all the girls who wanted to dance with me? Mom, I love girls!"

I smiled. The ratio of girls to boys had been about four to one. "I know, Nico. You were pretty popular today."

"Mom," Natalia said, "if I convert to Judaism, can I have a bat mitzvah too? I'm only eleven right now. I have time to prepare."

"Natis, you don't need to convert to have a party! We'll have a party when you do your Confirmation. It's the same concept as the Jewish bat mitzvah."

"Okay, Mami . . . don't forget you promised this." She laughed as we pulled into the driveway.

That December, the kids went over to the Amsels' to celebrate Hanukkah. They took and received presents and played dreidel, a traditional Hanukkah game played to celebrate the miracle that occurred with the candles in the temple of ancient Jerusalem. They came home laughing.

"Mami, we had a great time with the Amsels, and Christy was the winner with the dreidel," Nico said as they entered the house.

"Mami, I loved it!" Christy said. "We had so much fun, and Silvia always has amazing food. And they get eight days of presents!" She stared at our Christmas tree.

Sharing our religious traditions with others helped us learn to appreciate other people's beliefs. I am grateful that we met the Amsels at that point in our lives.

Silvia was full of wisdom. Whenever I had dating questions she would say, "Don't fight it. Things fall on their own."

Whenever I talked about raising kids and questioned my single-parenting skills, she would say, "It takes a village to raise a child. You are not alone."

Time after time, she had the phrase I needed to hear.

EPIPHANY

During the summer of 2007, I had almost no contact with Fernando, except minimal conversations relating to the children. They saw him weekly. Sometimes, they returned happy. Sometimes, they came home wishing he didn't drink.

He took them on small vacations. I felt left out and jealous that he could do things with them that I couldn't afford. I silently resigned myself to where I was in life. Whenever they were gone, the house felt empty and loneliness would creep back into my life. I was always concerned about whether he would be able to control his drinking around them. What gave me some relief was knowing he had a girlfriend who could help in those moments.

That summer, Christy went on a school trip. One day in July, she called me, crying. "Mami, I was at the Sacred Heart church in Montmartre, and I had an epiphany. I'm scared. I started crying, and this older priest came to me and told me, 'It will all be okay,' and blessed me. Mami, what is it?"

"What happened? What is an epiphany?" I asked, concerned.

"Something is going to happen, Mami." I heard her sniffle.

"Christy, whatever it is, we'll get through it together. Everything is okay at home. This is not the time to cry. Enjoy your trip and know that I love you." I put the phone down and went to look up the word *epiphany* on Wikipedia, wondering what it was all about.

"Epiphany: *(feeling)* an experience of sudden and striking insight."

I prayed out loud for protection. I've been blessed with a lot of intuition in my life, and I knew that if my daughter had felt something, it was real. When she returned home from her trip, we didn't think about the incident again. The children were happy; at that moment, life was filled with laughter.

A month later, we came to realize what she had foreseen about her father.

HOSPITAL

On August 7, 2007, Nicholas turned fifteen, and the expected highlight of his birthday was being able to get his driver's permit.

"Mami, it's my birthday today. Papi said he would take me to get my driver's permit, so I'm getting out of school early. I'm not going to spend the evening with you. But I'll call you when I have my permit so we can go driving today." Nicholas was so excited, he wore a big smile as he picked up his black backpack and ran toward the door to get in his friend's car.

"I'll be at work, so call me later. I'll pick you up there, and you can drive home." I watched him leave with pride.

Around two in the afternoon, I got a phone call at the office. It was Nicholas, who sounded exasperated and frustrated.

"Mami, Papi can't take me to get my driver's permit today. He keeps vomiting and then just goes back to bed. He keeps stumbling. He says he doesn't feel good and that he has the chills. He probably ate something that upset him and needs to sleep it off. Can you please come pick me up so I can get my permit?"

"What do you mean, he's vomiting and sleeping? What's going on?" I asked, concerned. I had a gut feeling that something wasn't right.

"I don't know, Mami; he just doesn't feel good. I called Daniel, and he said he would take me to his house to eat and can take me home later if you can't come, but I would really like to get my permit today."

"Nico, put Papi on the phone. I need to know what is going on with him."

"He can't come to the phone, Mami. He just wants to sleep," he answered, frustrated.

"Nico, don't leave. I'm coming over," I said frantically and put down the phone. I looked for Dr. Toro.

"Dr. Toro, I need to go. Something is wrong with Fernando. He's really sick. He's sleepy and vomiting everything up."

"Go," Dr. Toro said. "Call me if you need me. I'll see to your patients. And say hello to him for me." Dr. Toro had been Fernando's friend, and he knew our family. He knew a lot of things, actually, but prudence was a gift he had. He had never said a word that would hurt anyone.

I arrived at Fernando's house in thirty minutes, and when I saw him, I knew something was very wrong. He was pale, sweating, and shivering, and he could barely walk. Nicholas was with him.

"Mom, he's worse. He wasn't like this when I called you." Fear filled his voice.

I looked at Nico. "Help me get him in the car. I need to take him to the emergency room. He's probably dehydrated; he needs fluids."

As soon as we arrived at the hospital, they rushed him into a room. He was deteriorating rapidly. A lot of questions were asked, and they kept giving me paperwork. I was trying to remember everything I knew about his health, but I hadn't been around him for the last two years. I felt overwhelmed and scared.

The emergency doctor came into the room and rapidly asked questions, trying to get a history.

"How long has he been vomiting? Has he been febrile? Is anyone sick at home? What medicines does he take? We'll draw some blood, start an IV, and do an EKG. He's dehydrated, confused, and getting combative. Give me all the information you know so we can proceed as needed."

"I don't know how long he's been like this. He lives alone. He takes blood pressure medications, and he recently got diagnosed with rheumatoid arthritis. I called his doctor on the way here. He has had a couple of infusions for the arthritis. Do you think it's a bad case of gastroenteritis?" I asked, wondering what else could make him this sick.

"We'll know soon. We're sending out his labs stat, and we've started the IV." Then the doctor walked out.

I knew Fernando was getting worse, but I didn't know what was to come. Shortly after, the doctor returned and looked at me with concern.

"We need to transfer him to the medical center. He has acute pancreatitis and needs to be admitted into the ICU at Methodist. I'll get everything ready. You can ride in the ambulance. Just make arrangements for your car to be picked up, if needed."

I listened in disbelief. "Can I use my cell phone to make a call?"

"Of course. We're waiting for the ambulance."

I called Dr. Toro. "He has acute pancreatitis. They're transferring him to the ICU at Methodist. Every minute, he's getting worse. I won't be at work tomorrow." I started sobbing.

After a few minutes of silence, Dr. Toro said, "Don't worry about work. Take as long as you need. Fernando has a chronic illness. Call me when you get to the hospital. I'll have my phone with me at all times." Pancreatitis is an inflammation of the pancreas, one of the causes of which is heavy alcohol use, which Dr. Toro knew.

I was trying to remember everything I knew or had ever read about pancreatitis. There was a sense of urgency to get us out of the emergency room and into the ambulance. Fernando was sedated and on oxygen, and he was being infused with IV fluids as his vital signs were continually monitored.

Daniel had picked up Nicholas, so I called his father, Dr. Juan Gonzalez.

"Dr. Gonzalez, it's Pamela. I'm in an ambulance with Fernando. They're taking us to the ICU at Methodist for acute pancreatitis. I know you work there."

"Pam, I'll meet you all there. I won't say anything to Nicholas for right now. Let's see what is going on with Fernando first."

I didn't want Fernando to die. I had divorced him because of the drinking and the abuse, but he was still the father of my children. *Dear God, I don't know what to pray right now, but please help him. Please don't let him die.*

When we arrived at Methodist hospital, he was taken directly to one of the ICU rooms. Everything happened so quickly. The nursing staff worked in teams to hook him up to all the available monitors. When I saw his vital signs, I froze. In that moment, I knew he was dying, and I couldn't move.

I stared at the monitor, watching his vital signs drop, and then I looked at Fernando. I had worked in the ICU, so I knew what I was seeing. All the sounds were familiar: the nurses and doctors rushing, the organized chaos.

Finally, one of the nurses saw me and asked me to go to the waiting area while they stabilized him. She gently guided me to the family room. I sat outside and cried. I was alone, and my world was crumbling.

Dr. Gonzalez eventually came to talk to me. He stood beside me quietly.

"What is going on?" I asked, breaking the silence. "Tell me what's happening."

Measuring his words, he said, "He may not make it through the night. His organs are shutting down. I'm sorry. You need to stay, and we need to call the children."

I stared at him as he spoke.

"How much does he drink?" he asked, his expression full of concern. "And how long has he been an alcoholic?" Our children were best friends, yet I had kept this secret for years.

I cried as I answered. "It's a lot, and it's been a long time. But don't tell him I told you. He'll be angry, very angry."

I knew there was a high chance he wouldn't live through the night, but my legs were shaking. I was afraid of his reaction when he found out I had said he was an alcoholic. I had separated myself from it all, but now I was facing it again. The fear I had felt in the past had walked into my life again with that question.

"Does he know he has a drinking problem? Has he ever tried to stop?"

"He always denies it. He thinks he can take charge of his life at any time, but he can't. He's surrounded by people who will never challenge him, and if they ever do, he cuts them out of his life. I tried to do an intervention with his best friend and his sister, but nobody would support it. He refuses help."

"If he lives, he'll be told here that he needs help. He's very sick. He'll be put on dialysis in a little while. You need to stay here tonight. I'll be around." He held me as I cried.

The ICU doctor in charge came then to ask me the same questions Dr. Gonzalez had.

"How much does he drink? Has he ever tried treatment? We'll do everything we can, but he might not make it." Looking at me with a serious expression, he added, "Do you have children?"

"Yes, we have three."

"You may want to prepare them. Let's see how the night progresses." He walked away, and I turned to Dr. Gonzalez.

"It's late, and you don't want them driving at night. I'll send someone to pick them up if he deteriorates," he said, trying to console me.

Shortly after, I had visitors in the waiting room. Dr. Toro and his wife, Liliana, and Luz Maria and her husband, Rodrigo Mejia, had come to stay with me. They brought me food and a drink, but I couldn't eat. I just sat silently in their presence. It was comforting, though I felt numb.

I sat in the waiting room most of the night. I was allowed to see Fernando intermittently, but he was still balancing on the thin line between life and death. Around four in the morning, they finally came out to tell me that he was going to live. I breathed in relief as tears streamed down my face. I was grateful that my children still had a father.

The next morning, the children arrived for the first visiting hour. They hadn't been allowed to see him during the night because he had been so unstable. I prepared them for the visit. As they walked into the room, they all burst into tears. He was hooked up to every machine possible, was on dialysis, and was on oxygen. The monitor showed his blood pressure, heart rate, pulse, and oxygen levels. There was a continual rhythmic beeping as the IV fluids flowed drop by drop into his veins. He was pale, blending in with the sheets.

When the children started crying, Fernando's eyes fluttered, but he could barely open them. They sat silently by his bed, tears streaming down their cheeks. I felt a sharp stabbing in my heart from the pain of not being able to protect them from the reality they were living because of their father's illness.

Some things just have to be lived. When there is intense pain, only silence can bring comfort to the soul.

At that moment, I knew that whatever feelings I had had in the past, I needed to let them go. I wanted to be there for my children. In that ICU room, with my children surrounding their dying father, I made the choice to forgive and love him unconditionally for however long he had left to live. Forgiveness gave me freedom; it was a gift to myself. I forgave him for mistakes he'd made, and I forgave myself for mine.

Little by little, he got stronger. One evening, when I was in the ICU with him, Christina arrived alone. I could tell by the determined look on her face that she had come to speak with him. She sat beside him and held his hands as she cried angrily.

"Papi, Papi, why did you do this to yourself? Why did you destroy everything and everyone around you? We loved you. How could you get to this point? We were happy! You had us . . . you had everything. Why did you throw it away? Why did you throw us away? How could we not matter more? How could you put alcohol before us?"

He looked at her with tears in his eyes. "I'm sorry, Tina. I'm going to try, I really am . . . please, try to forgive me."

"You have a problem, Papi, and only you can fix it. I'm always going to love you because you're my father, and I'll forgive you. I want you to live. I want my dad alive, not dead."

I watched as my daughter's confrontation with her father made her stronger and brought her peace. I was very proud of her. At sixteen, she had faced her pain and addressed it. As a child, it was a huge breakthrough—telling her father the truth was not easy. Children often try to protect their parents and have difficulty confronting them, but that day, she found her voice.

Fernando stayed in the hospital for almost three weeks. It took a costly toll on his body, and he never completely regained his strength or his health. One evening, I was sitting by the bed when he asked me to put down the bedrail.

He gripped my hand. "Pamelita, I don't remember coming to the hospital or what happened that night, but I think I died."

I held his gaze. "I know you were between life and death, and they did everything except intubate you. That's the night they started dialysis. But why do you say that?"

"I went through a dark tunnel. It was cold—very, very cold." He paused for a while before continuing slowly. "It wasn't the light people talk about; it was different for me. I saw things about my life I'm ashamed of. I was cold, scared, and surrounded by darkness. I was going somewhere, but it wasn't where I wanted to go. I remembered that when I was a child, I believed and I prayed. I cried out a prayer—'Jesus, help me, forgive me'—and now I'm here. I believe I was given another chance."

I just listened. I had read about near-death experiences; usually, they were life changing. I believed him because I had been there that night. I silently said a prayer of thanksgiving before I responded, still holding his hand.

"Another chance is good. We only have one life, and you are still here." I wanted to say so much more, but the words just wouldn't come out. I silently remained by his side as he fell asleep holding my hand.

The nursing staff at Methodist were kind and compassionate. One day, before Fernando was discharged from the ICU to the floor, the nurse who was taking care of him asked me, "If he wants to die, why don't you let him?"

"Maybe he doesn't want to die. He has a family, and the children love him," I answered, not sure why he would ask me that.

There was silence in the room, then the nurse said kindly, "I've seen this before. People like him are usually hurting. Ask him what he wants before he comes back into the hospital again, because he probably will. Alcoholism is a chronic disease and a slow death."

I thanked him for his honesty. He had shared his experience. I knew it would continue to be a difficult battle for Fernando.

Before he was discharged from the hospital, I took the children to Carrabba's, our favorite restaurant for celebrating birthdays and special events. "Papi will be able to go home in a few days. He is going to need our help, so we need to plan ahead."

"Mami, as long as we can live in separate homes," Christy responded. "We can visit like before and help out more on weekends." Her siblings nodded in agreement.

"Okay, sounds good to me. He's going to try to not drink. He really wants to spend time with you all." I smiled encouragingly. The rest of dinner was spent talking and laughing. We all loved eating together as a family.

I had already set up some arrangements for part-time caregivers. The day we took Fernando to his home, Natalia sat by his side. "Papi, I don't care if you are sick. I want to build memories with you."

He held her hand and smiled. "I want the same, Natalia, I love you." He held her close.

He stopped drinking for five months, and it was perhaps some of the happiest times the children had ever had with him.

I had had a conversation with Dr. Toro at the hospital. I told him I couldn't go back to work for him. I wanted to help Fernando regain his health and had decided to help at his clinic. While still in the hospital, Fernando had told me he was going to close his clinic because he hadn't been able to sell it when he became aware his health was deteriorating. I asked him for the opportunity to buy it from him. Fernando would come daily for a few hours, using a cane or a walker, while I started working there alongside his nurse practitioner, Kat, as I got the paperwork ready for the sale.

Whenever he was asked about his hospitalization, Fernando would tell a story about a stomach virus that had attacked him and been so severe, he had developed sepsis. He used the medical terms to convince people. Only those with medical knowledge knew the truth. He had convinced himself that it wasn't his drinking. Alcohol was playing games with him, and once again, Alcohol was not to blame in his life.

In October that year, the day before his birthday, I was sitting in his office, paying bills, when he approached me. He had his cane and was walking slowly. I looked up at him and smiled.

"Fernando, I have the attorney's papers ready for the sale. I'm just waiting for a loan approval." I calmly showed him the papers.

The look on his face changed. He grabbed the papers and threw them on the floor. He raised his voice angrily. "I am the owner of this clinic. You are my employee, and I will never sell this clinic to you. You're fired. FIRED! Take all your things and leave."

My blood boiled, my face felt hot, and my legs shook as I stood up and looked at him. I stared for a few minutes and took deep breaths. "You will never scream at me again. I left my job because we had an agreement, and I came to help you. But I'm leaving now. I will not allow you to treat me this way."

He turned around, slammed the door, and left the clinic. Immediately, I packed all my belongings in a box and left through the back door. I was shaken, but not beaten. I had left before; this was just another game.

I didn't say a word to the children when I got home. It was Fernando's birthday the next day, and they had promised him that we would take him to Buca di Beppo to eat. I went with them and met him there. I wished him a happy birthday and sat and ate. I did not exchange any other words with him; it wasn't necessary. I had promised to help with his care, but I would draw the line on the behaviors. He celebrated his fifty-first birthday with his family, the children laughed and ate, and we went home happy that night.

The next morning, I got up and went to a yoga class. I had lost my job, but I had some savings. I wasn't desperate like I had been previously. At first, I didn't tell the children I had been fired. Instead, I walked, I wrote, and I prayed for guidance.

One evening in November, Christina said, "Mami, I want to go to Bikram Yoga with you at five o'clock, before school. Can I join you?"

"Of course, but it gets pretty hot in there." She hated steam rooms, but that didn't deter her.

We started going together, but after two weeks, she said, "Mami, I'm exhausted all day and want to sleep through all my classes. How do you do it?"

I laughed. "Well, I come home and sleep after yoga."

"What about work, Mom? Don't you start at eight?"

"I didn't tell you, but I got fired from the clinic last month. I'm looking for a job."

"You what? Why didn't you tell us, Mami?" She waved her hands, flustered.

"It happened the day before Papi's birthday. You all were so excited about going out to dinner with him that I felt that was more important at the time. It's the memories you create that you remember throughout life. I'm okay. I just needed some time alone, and I'm getting it."

I hugged her and laughed. I was looking again, and I hoped to start working by January 2008.

Fernando invited the children to go to Colombia with him during their Christmas break. They were excited and happy to spend time with him, especially since he hadn't been drinking at night while they were together.

They left for Colombia on December 21, 2007. Meanwhile, I had planned a Christmas yoga retreat with my mother in

California. It was a retreat filled with silent activities: meditation, yoga classes, long hikes, and journaling. Conversations were only allowed in the evenings. Meals were the most difficult; we made eye contact and smiled at those sharing our table. The first day was exhausting, but we got used to it. My mom and I laughed more than we had in years. Silence and prayer gave me strength, but holidays without my children were still painful.

On Dec 29, 2007, I was back in Houston when the telephone rang. It was seven in the evening.

"Mom, come pick us up. We just got back from Colombia. He's drinking again." There was sadness in Christy's voice. My heart sank.

"Where are you guys? Are you at home?" I ran to get my car keys.

"Yeah, we just arrived at Papi's house, and he's already drinking. Please come pick us up," she said urgently.

"I'm on my way."

Arriving at his house, I rang the bell. When they opened the door, they were ready. They silently hugged, tears in their eyes. They had each written him a letter, and they left them on the breakfast table.

"Mami, he promised he wouldn't, but he started the third day we were there. Why did he do that?" Natalia questioned angrily, holding onto my arm.

"It's an illness, Natis. He tried to beat it, but it's stronger than him." I had known how difficult this battle would be for him and the high incidence of remission. But everyone's hopes had been high.

I took them home, and we made hot chocolate. We did what we had always done in these situations: we all slept together and held each other. It was another broken promise in their life. Another wound to heal.

Three days later, I received a phone call from Fernando.

"I know the kids are angry. I tried, but it's stronger than I am."

His unusual humility shocked me, and I was silent for a while. I knew he had tried, and I knew it would kill him eventually. But it surprised me that he was telling me this. He had never admitted weakness before.

"I'm sorry. Do you want outside help?" I asked.

"No. I'm tired. I want to sell you the clinic," he said.

"We've already gone down this road, and I don't want the emotional roller coaster in my life," I answered calmly. "Anyways, I can't get a loan. I have no credit. I'm looking for a steady job right now."

"It's different this time," he said in a low voice. "There's a lien on the clinic; if I don't pay it off, I'll lose the clinic. I love my patients. Help me keep it going. I'll finance it for you. You can pay me month by month. If you don't do this, I'll have to close it down."

It has to be bad if he's reaching out to me like this, I thought. It was the break I needed to run my own clinic.

I smiled. "I'm in, but only if I can change the name of the clinic. I want it to be Clinica La Salud. That was the name I chose last year, but we never finished the paperwork."

"The name is not a problem," he said, "but I want you to keep the staff. They have families. Let's meet and start making arrangements. I'll have my attorney draw up the documents."

"Thank you for the opportunity, Fernando. I can't wait to tell the kids." I hung up the phone.

That evening, I prepared another of our traditions.

"Guess what we're having for dinner tonight," I said excitedly once everyone was home.

"Colombian food," Natalia guessed gleefully.

"Not today. We are having our French dinner! I bought all

165

types of cheeses, different cuts of meat, and baguettes. All we need are candles. We are celebrating tonight!"

They stared at me, waiting for the news.

"I have a job. But it gets better. I'm buying the clinic from Papi!" I said with a sense of accomplishment.

"Wow, Mami, that's great news, but can you afford it?" asked Christina.

"He's going to finance it," I said happily.

It was a deal that worked for both of us. Our relationship had evolved to one of friendship. It had taken several years to get to this place in life, but I had finally arrived.

At my yoga retreat, I had met a man who became my friend and mentor. It was a long-distance relationship, but it brought joy to my life. While I wasn't looking to get married, I enjoyed the intellectual conversations, the monthly visits, and the exploration of new restaurants whenever he visited. By that time in my life, I enjoyed my time alone. Life seemed to be flowing smoothly.

LOSS

In February 2008, I had a complete hysterectomy.
I had been suffering from chronic abdominal pain and cramping and had been bleeding for the past year. Before my yoga retreat, I had had a vaginal ultrasound done. When I returned, I received a phone call from my doctor

"Pam, I need you to come into the office tomorrow. We need to talk about your ultrasound results."

"Yes, of course. Can you tell me what's wrong over the phone?" I asked, concerned.

"We need to schedule you for surgery. I'll explain tomorrow in detail, but don't worry about it right now."

"You know my situation. Am I going to be okay? My kids need me."

"It isn't life threatening, but you do need surgery. There's a mass on your uterus that we need to remove." the doctor explained.

I went into surgery the next week. My mother, Silvia, and Anne took turns staying with me and helping me with meals. The kids came to visit every day after school. Nicholas sat by my bed silently, holding my hand. The first day, he didn't say a word.

The second day he visited, he walked in cheerfully. "Mami, I spoke with the nurse, and you need to walk. Let's do it together."

He made me walk up and down the hallways, holding the IV pole, until I regained my strength enough to go home. He was always ready to hold me if I fell.

I didn't tell Fernando I was having surgery. I had made the decision while he was out of town, and I didn't want him there. I finally called him after the surgery.

"I'm in the hospital. I had a hysterectomy two days ago, but I'm recovering."

"Where are you? I'll come and visit," he said, sounding distressed.

"Methodist in Sugar Land. Room 302," I answered without much strength.

Fernando came to visit that day, using a walking cane. "Why didn't you tell me you were having surgery?" he asked me angrily.

"You've been out of town for the past two weeks, and the doctor said it was urgent."

"I would have canceled my trip to be here and help."

"I didn't want you to worry."

"You should have told me! I needed to be here for the kids," he responded, still upset.

I didn't have the strength to fight back. I closed my eyes and prayed for a fast recovery. His visit had reminded me why we couldn't be together. I needed to live and get out of the hospital.

That night, I had a vivid dream that I would later share with the children. It began with me in a dark room, surrounded by black flying creatures who were trying to suffocate me. They took the form of bats, but they weren't bats. I couldn't see their faces, but I felt them surrounding me. My heart raced, and I looked around, terrified. I started making the sign of the cross and saying, "I am not afraid. I am a child of God. The Lord is my shepherd; I shall not fear."

I continued this as I looked all around the room. As I repeated the prayer, the creatures started disappearing. Then I saw a little child dressed in white, their face glowing face as they held out a hand for me to take. We walked from the dark room into a space filled with light. An incredible sense of peace and love filled me. I was not afraid anymore.

I woke up the next day, and I knew my life had taken a different road. I realized the frailty of the soul and how the environment I had been in had torn at me.

In 2008, Fernando moved from the suburbs to the city. He bought a townhouse close to the I-610 loop near Richmond and painted it yellow.

"Papi, that's a very bright yellow," Natalia said, laughing, when we went to visit.

"Yes, the neighbors hate it and complained, but I don't care. This way, you can find me in the neighborhood." He laughed.

His health continued to deteriorate throughout the year. His rheumatoid arthritis had gotten worse, and he had begun to suffer from bouts of gout. Pain became a constant presence in his life. His mobility decreased; he stopped walking without assistance, and a wheelchair became his silent companion. Christy and Nicholas were driving by then, so it was easier for them to visit him since they could leave if needed.

In December 2008, Fernando called me. "I want to take the kids to Colombia for Christmas. I'm too sick to go alone . . . I want you to come with us, so I can be with them."

"Are you sure about this?" I asked. "What will the sleeping arrangements be?"

"You and the kids stay in one hotel room, and I'll stay in another. I really want to go, but I don't want them to have to handle me and the wheelchair alone." He spoke calmly, his voice sincere.

"Have you talked to them about this already?"

"No, I wanted to ask you first," he said slowly. "I need your help. It would mean a lot to me, but I understand if you don't want to."

I remained silent as I decided. I loved Colombia and hadn't been for several years. I made up my mind quickly.

"If they want to go, I'll go. They want to spend time with you, and we can make it work."

Being around him for a week, I realized he was losing ground fast. It was a trip filled with laughter and nostalgia. The children were happy to be with both of us, and at night, the children and I went to our room and he to his. Alcohol kept him company, but the lack of mobility kept him in his room.

We returned to Houston after New Year's Day, and school resumed. Everything seemed to be back to normal until the last week in January, when I got a call from Fernando's caretaker.

"Señora, I think you need to come to the doctor's house now. He's shaking, and something is not right."

I left the clinic immediately. When I arrived, he was lying on the sofa. He was pale and diaphoretic. His shirt was damp, and he was clammy.

He was barely alert, but when he saw me, he said, "I don't want to go to the hospital."

"You don't look good. You're white as a ghost. I'm calling your doctor."

"Please, I don't want to go. Leave me at home," he begged as he closed his eyes.

I made the call and rapidly explained the situation to the nurse who answered.

"If he's that sick," she replied, concerned, "you need to take him to the hospital or call an ambulance. Do you have an out-of-hospital do-not-resuscitate order?"

"No, I don't." I didn't know where any of Fernando's legal papers were.

"Then call the ambulance or take him to the hospital. Avoid giving yourself a headache in the future. It's the best advice I can give you. If he wants to die at home, he needs to have the paperwork ready." She spoke the words matter-of-factly.

As I hung up, he started seizing, and I dialed 911. He was hospitalized with gastrointestinal bleeding. Death was hovering around him, patiently waiting. He was there for a week before being discharged to go home.

His strength was gone, and he needed to be carried from the wheelchair, to the couch, to the bed. I hired full-time caretakers to help with him. The children and I were there in the evenings and on weekends. I remembered the promise I had made in 2007. We would take care of him, but we would never move back in together. It was what kept us sane.

One weekend in February, I called Christina during her Confirmation retreat.

"Christy, you need to come. Papi's not doing well. He's having seizures again, but this time, he's not responding as well."

"I brought my car," she said. "I told them my dad was sick, so I'll be there soon."

Father Phil, the priest for St. Theresa's, where Christina was preparing to be confirmed, found out she had to leave and came to visit Fernando that evening. Nicholas was at the house and opened the door when Father Phil arrived.

"Hello, Nicholas! I came to visit your dad." Father Phil smiled as he spoke in his British accent.

Nicholas was shocked. He couldn't believe it was him. He stood at the door for a while before finally responding.

"Yes, Father, I'll take you to my dad." He led the priest to Fernando.

Father Phil started visiting weekly and bringing communion.

Sometimes, the children and I would be there, and at other times, it was just the two of them.

One day, he came while I was pushing Fernando's wheelchair through the neighborhood. Fernando had a glass of whiskey in one hand. As soon as Father Phil approached us, Fernando put the glass in my hand.

"Hello, Fernando, pretty day for a walk," Father Phil said, pretending he hadn't seen the glass. "I'll spend a little time with you."

"Yes, Father. Drinking some water right now. It's hot outside." Fernando smiled and hid his trembling hands.

Father Phil walked with us around the corner and then spent some time alone with him.

It didn't matter anymore if he drank or not. That was where he was in life. I had seen Fernando fight with God and the Church for years, yet Father Phil's visits brought him peace. He asked for the sacraments he could receive and always looked forward to communion. The fight against alcohol was no longer worth fighting.

I wrote Christy's senior retreat letter from him while he was in the hospital during one of his admissions.

"Fernando, it's Christy's senior retreat. What do you want to say to her?" I kept asking gently. "They want the parents to write something."

"I've fought many battles, and most of them were not worth it. Don't fight." He kept repeating those last words over and over, as well as saying he loved her.

After his third admission to the hospital, I asked about hospice, as Fernando had requested. As I did, I kept hold of his hand.

"Doctor, can you please write an order for hospice. Fernando has voiced over and over that he doesn't want any more doctor visits or hospitalizations. We've already called the ambulance three times this year. He continues losing weight, and he's down to one hundred pounds now."

"Fernando, is that what you want?" the doctor asked, leaning over and sitting beside him.

"Yes. I just want to stay home. I don't want this life. Look at me. I'm wasting away. I don't want to fight anymore to live." He looked up at the doctor from his wheelchair, tears streaming down his face.

Hospice would allow Fernando to die with dignity. It also allowed my children to see death as a natural part of life. It took away the fear.

"I saw my dad walking with me today," he told me one evening as he lay in bed.

"Were you happy to see him?" I asked.

"Yes, I was. He was holding my hand," he said peacefully.

I knew death was approaching and called a psychologist I had seen after the divorce to help prepare the children.

Fernando continued to fill his Ensure bottles with whiskey, but we didn't care anymore, or perhaps we were kinder. He experienced moments of dementia when he relived his childhood, the children's early years, and his professional life. If he thought we were on a trip, we would put his suitcase in the car and drive him around the neighborhood.

"It's time to go!" he would say excitedly. "We need to pack the suitcases. Hurry, hurry!"

"Mami, let's go! All the suitcases are ready!" Nico would say.

Everyone went along. It was a game we played.

He was always happy when we did this because he thought we had just come back from a trip.

Several weeks before he died, he was visited by an old friend and his wife. While they visited, the wife approached me. "Do you believe in reincarnation?"

"I don't know," I answered. "I hope when I die, I'll go to heaven. It'd be pretty hard having to come back."

"Pam, you have to cross his legs when he dies. The soul has to leave through the head, not the bottom part of his body. If you don't cross his legs, he'll reincarnate and still have affairs. If you're with him in the next life, it will all be the same." Both her voice and her eyes were filled with concern.

I stared at her in disbelief. "Where did that come from?"

"I've been reading a lot about death and dying. You might end up with him again. If you want faithfulness, cross his legs. The soul needs to leave through the head!"

It was a thought that stayed with me.

During the second week in April, I signed my mom and sisters up for a meditation retreat at Rice University.

"Pamelita, why can't we just go to the movies?" Cynthia complained. "Where do you find these strange events? We have to sit on the floor with our eyes closed and breathe. It's boring."

I laughed. "It will be fun, and we'll be together."

"I don't think this is fun," she said, looking me in the eye. Later, when lunch came, she complained again. "Pamelita, this is really weird, but worst of all is the food. It's all vegetarian. I'm not a rabbit! I like meat!"

That time, Elizabeth answered. "Hey, Cynthia, it's about the meditation. I love all this stuff, and you know we need to eat healthily. We can get a Snickers bar when we leave!"

After lunch, we all settled back into lotus position and closed our eyes. Cynthia was trying to stop giggling as the leader kept telling us to breathe in and out. Suddenly, I had the urge to leave. A thought came into my mind: *the children need to talk to Fernando now.* I got up and told my sisters and the teacher that I had to leave at that moment. As I got in the car, I called them all.

"Christy, Nico, Natis, meet me at Papi's house. It's important."

"What's wrong, Mami?" Natalia asked. "We just saw him this morning. He's probably sleeping right now."

"I'll tell you when we get there. Just meet me at his house," I said firmly.

Fifteen minutes later, after we'd all arrived at his house, I told them my experience during meditation.

"You need to tell him everything you want to right now. Also, listen and forgive. It's time to say what is in your hearts."

One by one, they sat by his bed and, with tears in their eyes, exchanged words of love and forgiveness. Years later, I would read the book *The Four Things That Matter Most* by Dr. Ira Byock, a hospice doctor. Those four things are the following phrases: "Thank you," "I love you," "Please forgive me," and "I forgive you." I knew then that the time my children had spent sitting by their father had been a blessing in their lives.

His last month was filled with unbearable suffering. Every movement caused severe pain. On April 27th, Natalia left on her eighth-grade trip to Washington, DC. It was something she had looked forward to. It was her fourteenth birthday, and I had thought it would be good for her to celebrate with this trip. Fernando had also wanted her to go.

He kept saying, "Go on your trip. I'll be right here when you get back."

I took Natalia to the airport and kissed her goodbye, reminding her of her dad's promise.

At noon, I got a call from Fernando's caretaker, telling me he had a fever of 103. I ran over to see him and called hospice.

The nurse told me, "It's getting closer. We've talked about what you need to do. Above all, stay calm."

I called the schools and told them I needed the children home. I frantically worked with Duchesne to get Natalia back to Houston.

On Wednesday morning, he opened his eyes and looked at me.

"Fernando, please, not now," I pleaded. "Natalia will be arriving at the airport any moment now. Please wait for her."

He had been unconscious since Monday. He gave me a long look, closed his eyes again, and continued to breathe. I helped the nurse as much as I could.

Natalia arrived shortly after. We all stayed in his room, monitoring his progress.

The next day, April 30th, Christy woke up. "Papi, it's my birthday today. I know you can hear me. It's my eighteenth birthday today."

I had already bought a birthday cake for Christina. At noon, he opened his eyes and looked at me again. I was alone with him at that moment, but I knew it was time. I called the children into the room.

"Christy, Nico, Natis, Mom, come, come now. Papi is awake; we need to say goodbye."

They all rushed into the room and sat around the bed.

"Let's turn on the Gregorian chants," I instructed. "He loved those when we were younger. Let's also start the rosary. Tell him you love him. He can hear us."

The hospice nurse had told me that people die the way they lived their life. Fernando had an active death. He struggled to breathe, but during this time, he kept looking at the children. I followed all the hospice recommendations to make it as peaceful as possible, but it was still an agonizing death.

He died at the age of fifty-two on April 30th at 12:25 p.m., surrounded by his family. I believe God received him with open arms. I felt God's grace in his life.

A few minutes after his last breath, I told the children, "His soul is still here. Let's put his favorite red shirt on him and celebrate Christy's birthday with Papi."

We dressed him up and brought the candle-ladened cake into the room. As we sang "Happy Birthday," the doorbell rang.

"I don't know who it could be," I said. "I haven't called anyone yet."

His caretaker went to open the door. Father Phil walked slowly into the room to find us all around Fernando's body, cutting the cake.

"It's my birthday, Father Phil, and I wanted Papi to be part of it," Christy whispered.

"I think I will also have a piece of cake," the priest said, smiling as he pulled up a chair.

After a while, I called hospice, and they notified the funeral home. When they arrived, they stated, "We're here to remove the body."

Father Phil immediately stepped in. "You are here to pick up Fernando, and this is his family who loved him."

They immediately apologized. "Yes, we're here for Fernando. Take the time you need; we'll wait."

The children broke down crying as they said their final goodbyes to Fernando.

Father Phil held Natalia in his arms and comforted her as she sobbed.

"Father Phil, a lot of people didn't love my dad, but I loved him. Can we have the love passage from Corinthians at the funeral? I want to read it."

"Yes, Natalia, we can," he responded as he held her.

Since Fernando had first gotten sick, I had come to appreciate Silvia Amsel's support not only of me but of the children. She had become an aunt to them. The day before Fernando's funeral, she dropped by the house.

"I brought you some food," she said, unloading several trays unto the kitchen counter. When she had finished putting them all away, she smiled at me. "What can I help you with? These

177

are difficult moments, so you need to use me right now. Allow me to help."

I sat down and looked at her. "Can you take Natalia shopping for a funeral dress?"

"Yes, I'll take care of that. Now eat something. You need to keep your strength up."

That night, my brother Juan and his wife, Elsa, came over to visit. We were still at Fernando's house. I had not seen them in eight years. They came by unannounced, but when I saw my brother, I knew the love between us was as strong as it had always been. Nothing was said about the past, nothing was questioned, and nothing needed to be said. They were there to support us.

That was the beginning of our healing with family and friends. Fernando had loved and hated, helped and destroyed, lived with intensity and passion. Slowly, all the friends I had loved for years reentered my life: Luz Maria, Maru, Gisela, Maria, Juliana, my tennis friends, and all the others. I had pulled away from them when I left in 2005. I had needed space and time to heal. My heart had been ashamed, broken, and afraid. I put distance between myself and a lot of people. As I look at my life now, I don't know if that was right or wrong, but it was what I needed to heal.

At the funeral, I was shocked by all the faces I saw and the outpouring of love that I felt. Maybe with the passage of time, people who were harmed by his actions were able to forgive him. I was a small part of his life. However, I received the greatest gift ever given to me, my children, and I will always be grateful for that.

His funeral took place on Tuesday, May 5, 2009, at St. Theresa's at Memorial Park. The service was presided over by Father Phil. Natalia stood up to do the second reading, my mother at her side.

Her voice quivered as she began. "Love is patient, love is kind . . ."

As the mass finished, I walked up to the lectern and looked at my children who sat in the front pew of the church. They knew that what I was about to read was for them.

"Gracias, Dr. Toro, por el apoyo constante con Fernando, conmigo, y con los niños. Gracias a todos sus pacientes de la clínica. Ustedes eran familia.

"Thank you, Daniel, Alan, and Andres, for being there for Nicholas. Thank you, Rachel, for your constant presence in Natalia's life. To the Amsel, Gonzalez, and García families, your presence has been a constant reminder of angels. Thank you for loving my children.

"Thank you, Kathleen and Sonia, for the unconditional love and loyalty you had for Fernando. You were his rocks at difficult times in the clinic.

"Virginia, he knew you loved him. You were his sister. Thank you for visiting him and loving him.

"Thank you, hospice, for allowing Fernando to die at home, surrounded by his children. Thank you, Cynthia and Juan Carlos, for loving my children. For your acceptance and your constant kindness.

"Monita, words can never express your support over the years. Your weekly phone calls, your love. You have always been there. Thank you for your unconditional love.

"Mother, thank you for helping us take care of Fernando, for taking him daily communion, and for just sitting beside him and holding his hand in his agony. You have been our example throughout our lives. This would not have been possible without you.

"Fernando, thank you for life beside you. We did a full circle, and I thank you for this. Love never dies; it just transforms itself. I want you to go in peace, knowing your children will be in good hands.

"Christina, Nicholas, and Natalia, it is never easy to lose a parent, and it is more difficult when you are young. Papi always loved you. Sometimes, he just didn't know how to show it. He accomplished great things, but he was also human and had great struggles. Life with Papi was a roller coaster: He made us laugh, and he made us cry. He was unpredictable, yet his love for you all was unconditional. As parents, we make many mistakes, sometimes hurting those we love the most. You have faced many challenges in these last years, and I am proud of how you have handled them. When Papi got sick a year and a half ago, each one of you started helping out. The past was left behind. The present was his situation.

"Christy, I remember how excited you were about being a senior and wanting to spend time with friends and have fun. Yet as his health deteriorated, you started spending less time with friends and more with him. From a few hours a week, it became days. It was a sacrifice of love. I know how much you wanted him to see you and Natalia graduate, yet you told him it was okay if he had to let go because you didn't want him to continue to hurt. He read your letter and cried because you gave him permission. Thank you for giving him peace.

"Nicholas, you started spending weekend nights with your father to help him ambulate, to carry him to his bed and to his sofa. Since you are stronger than your sisters, you did a lot of the carrying. You planned your weekend schedule around his needs. He couldn't move until we came; he couldn't eat until we brought food. Thank you for loving him. Thank you for the dignity with which you treated him.

"Natalia, you loved him and cared for him. You told him a year and a half ago that you wanted memories with him, and you cared for him with gentleness. You would sit down and tell him about your school, your friends, and your teachers. When he was in the hospital, you never wanted to leave his side. You knew how difficult it was for him to go to your Father-Daughter Mass, and you made him feel special. He knew how much you wanted your eighth-grade trip, and he kept his last promise to you. He waited for you to come back from Washington. Thank you for your kindness and your gentleness with him.

"I love you all. Thank you for loving him, for making him laugh, for holding his hand, for standing up for your beliefs, for carrying him when he couldn't walk, for silence when he was hurting, for your presence when he was dying. You treated him with dignity. You taught him the greatest lesson in life. You taught him that what was really important in life was not greatness but forgiveness and love.

"Fercito, go in peace. Know always that your family loves you."

Before we left the church that day, Father Phil approached me and held my hands. "You did the right thing for you and the children. Women are not meant to be doormats."

In the weeks that followed, Christina graduated from high school and Natalia from eighth grade. From that day forward, Father Phil became another family member. Over the years, he has shared their lives and participated in their celebrations. He is family to all of us.

LETTER

I have been thinking about sadness and how it influences our lives. It comes silently into the heart, at times uninvited. It is not a bad feeling if we recognize it for what it is: an emotion to get us back on our feet. If it stays for long, it takes our energy away. Sadness for relationships that are on hold, sadness for relationships that have ended, sadness for the loss of someone loved, sadness for unwanted situations.

It is not a feeling I am unfamiliar with, for at times in my life it has been a companion. It is because of this that I recognize it when it comes to visit. I let it stay for short periods of time, and then I walk it out the door. This is not easy but necessary, for life is to be embraced with gratitude and not sadness.

So, my beautiful people, I have a list of things that will help you all when this feeling comes to visit and wants to stay in your heart . . .

Love,
Mami

RETURN TO COLOMBIA

That summer, we arranged a trip to Colombia with his ashes, and those of his parents, which had been in his closet for eight years. We held a small mass with his high school friends and family at Iglesia Santa Bibiana in Bogotá, and his ashes were placed under the church in the mausoleum. The next day, we went to Santa Marta with Cynthia and my mother.

The day we flew to Colombia, Nicholas picked up my mom. "G-ma, make sure you have your suitcase."

"Nicholas, I'm always prepared. Elsa and I packed everything this week, and it is all color coordinated," she said with a proud smile.

Before we left the house, I asked again, "Does everyone have their suitcase? Make sure you have your things. Mom, do you have everything?"

"Yes, Mami. Everyone is ready," Natalia replied. My mom nodded confidently.

When we arrived at the airport, everyone unloaded the car. Suddenly, my mother asked, "Where is my suitcase? Who has my suitcase?

"Grandma, I asked you if you had your suitcase," Nicholas said, looking at her.

"I put it in the white car when you picked me up," she answered anxiously.

"Grandma . . . we changed cars to come to the airport. You didn't move your suitcase?" he asked, surprised.

"What am I going to do? I need to go back for my clothes."

"Mom, we don't have time to go back," I said. "We'll miss the flight. We'll just buy what you need once we get to Colombia."

"Please, let's not ever talk about this. Elsa helped me pack for a week, and I don't want her to know this happened," Mom said nervously.

We would keep that secret for several years. One day, though, at dinner with the cousins, it would be revealed, bringing lots of laughter to everyone there.

We spent a week in Santa Marta with Elizabeth, who lived in Colombia with her family. We took long beach walks daily and had five-dollar body massages on the beach. We had also planned day trips. One day, we learned about a tour for a healing hot springs, which included mud baths and massages. We all decided to go.

"Let's do this tour. We get lunch, and we get to soak in hot water," I told the kids.

"Yes, Mami! It will be like a spa day," Christy said happily.

When we arrived, we saw two small huts, a large open field, and a lot of hot springs.

"Come on, guys! Let's get into the healing waters, and then we can get mud massages," I said excitedly.

We spent the evening there and took turns getting massages. We took pictures when we all got into the hot, smelly muddy pond. Our whole bodies were covered with mud.

That evening, everyone had diarrhea.

"Mom, maybe that wasn't the best idea today. We're all sick," Natalia said, running to the bathroom.

Several months after the trip, Christina would mention her boyfriend, who had gone with us to Colombia.

"Mom, do you know he still has diarrhea? It started after our mud bath."

"You mean in Colombia?" I ask incredulously. "Why didn't he tell me? It's probably parasites or amoebas. I'll call in a prescription for metronidazole for him."

His diarrhea was resolved in a week.

LETTER

Parenting is not easy. Christy, Nicholas, and Natalia, you have been my greatest blessings in life. I know that I have made a lot of mistakes as a parent, and I ask your forgiveness for the times I didn't pay attention, the times I didn't understand, and the times I was not there. Only with the passage of time do we truly value the gift of a newborn who turns our lives upside down, as you three did to mine. I want you to know, I tried my best.

We have truly had a beautiful life together. I remember each pregnancy, each birth, each birthday, and all the tears and laughter we have shared. This is your world and your life. Make the most out of every moment you live. Our biggest gift to each other is the time we have together. You will discover that time together is precious.

Mami

MOVING ON

In the summer of 2009, after we had returned from Colombia, we purchased two raclette grills and started having interactive dinners. We would place the grills on the tabletop, and everyone would cook and talk at the same time. The kids' friends loved coming over to eat. There were many nights of laughter and conversation over cheese, meats, chicken, potatoes, and toast.

"Where's the cheese?" Christy would say. "Make sure you don't take all the shrimp."

"I call the potatoes," someone else would answer.

"Pass me the chimichurri sauce."

"The cheese is melted just perfect."

"My toast is ready."

Through previous years, we had set the rules of the house. Besides chores, everyone had a night they cooked. Natalia loved rosemary chicken dishes. Nicholas got away with quesadillas and experimented with new dishes with his friend, Alan, who wanted to be a chef at the time. It was Christina, however, who was always looking at recipes on her phone and coming up with new dishes.

One evening, Christina said, "I'm having a special dinner for everyone today, and I want everyone to dress up."

"What are you cooking?" Natalia asked. "I want to help."

"Not tonight, Natis. It's my turn, and I'm making a special

dinner for all of you. I already bought all the ingredients." She had a big smile on her face.

Looking at the kitchen counter, I saw kosher salt, jalapeños, rice, fish, and different curry spices I had never seen before.

"Okay, I'll set the table while you cook. That way, we all have time to dress up," Natalia said as she started helping. When dinner was ready, we all gathered around the table.

"Bless the food, Christy," I said. "You cook, you bless. We're all looking forward to your new creation." After the blessing, we all looked at her, and I offered her a big smile. "Tell us about the dishes."

"These recipes were under the colorful, spicy, and healthy meals. Taste it and see if it's delicious," Christina urged. We all reached for our forks and took our first bites, then immediately reached for our water glasses. Nicholas broke the silence.

"Yuck! This sucks."

"What's wrong? What is it, Nico?" Christina asked, looking surprised.

"The green rice is a little too spicy. What did you put in it?" I asked before drinking more water to soothe my throat.

"It's green rice, Mami. The recipe called for a quarter jalapeño, but I thought it wasn't enough, so I just added a little more."

"How much more?" My eyes were tearing from the burning sensation on my tongue.

"I put in a whole one. Is it too spicy?"

"A little. What about the seeds? Did you remove them?" I asked.

"No, I just added the whole jalapeño—"

"Christy," Nico interrupted, "this is really nice of you, but the fish is really, really salty also."

"I added extra kosher salt to it. I didn't think it had enough." Tears had begun to pool in her eyes.

"I think you need to taste the food as you go, or it can get a little strong," I said gently as we all pushed our plates to the side.

"I worked so hard and wanted it to be special," she said, crying.

"It's special that you did this for us, but it's just too hot." I gave her a hug. "Let's just pass on this meal and go get Mexican food, but don't let me drink a margarita. I love them, but they make me sick."

Preparing meals and eating together brought a lot of laughter and memories into our lives.

Slowly, our life returned to a steady rhythm of work and play.

In August, my mom and I drove Christina to Duke University, where she had been accepted for college.

"Mami, I will be back," she told me sternly. "Don't let Natalia move into my room."

"Of course not. It's your room." I hugged her goodbye and started crying.

Within a few weeks, Natalia approached me with a big smile. "Mami, since Christy isn't living with us anymore and her closet is bigger, I want to switch rooms."

"Natis, I just promised her you wouldn't do that."

"Mami, she's not here! She won't know."

"Natalia, we can't do that yet. She's in college, but she will be back for breaks. It's too soon. Let's wait on that."

Natalia never asked to move again.

I missed Christina's presence, but her being away at college gave me more time with Nicholas and Natalia. That was when I realized that, someday, they would all have their own lives.

That year, Nicholas started his junior year of high school. One night, he walked into my room and started the following conversation.

"Mami, I have always wanted to be a soccer player. Remember how angry I got at you for not sending me to high school in Spain so I could play soccer?"

"Yes. I remember that," I replied, looking at him curiously.

"I want to be a doctor, Mami. I've been thinking a lot about that lately."

"A doctor? You can do it; where there's a will, there's a way. Are you ready for a lot of reading?" I asked, knowing what it takes.

"I do, Mami, and I will." He hugged me and smiled as he walked out of the room. Nicholas would eventually fulfil his dream and get his MD in 2019. He continued to play soccer throughout his college years.

Whenever we had the house to ourselves, Natalia and I found new activities to do together. On Friday nights, we would curl up on the couch, watching movies and eating popcorn. On Saturday mornings, we went bike riding.

One day, she said to me, "Mami, we should dress up and go to a nice restaurant together once a month. It will be our date nights."

"It sounds like fun," I agreed. "Let's start tonight."

"Mami, if I say it's my birthday, I'll get a free dessert. It works all the time." She smiled as she said it. That night, we began our monthly outings. She picked the restaurants, we dressed up, and as she'd predicted, dessert was always free.

Fernando's death brought peace and paperwork. There was peace in knowing that suffering had ceased for another human being, but I was not prepared to deal with the amount of work that death brought. Lawyers, accountants, hospital bills, credit card statements . . . the list went on. I was overwhelmed until my friend Silvia told me, "Do them one by one. Don't tackle everything at once."

Soon after Fernando's death, I realized there was a big difference for women between being widowed and being divorced. How unjust and unfair it is, yet it's true. Society feels compassion for widows, which is rarely offered to divorcées.

I visited Christy at Duke for Parents' Weekend in October. As we walked through the Duke gardens, holding hands, she asked me, "Mami, do you want to get married again?"

"I don't know. If I do, I hope it's before I'm fifty. I don't think I would remarry after that; I'm too happy being alone." We both laughed.

"Mami, when I get married, I'll have a small wedding so it's not too expensive for you."

I stopped and smiled at her. "Christy, if I get married again, I am throwing a huge party with a big dance!"

She giggled. "Mami, I was trying to be nice! If you have a big wedding, then I want a big one too!"

When I returned to Houston, I looked around for dance classes. I signed Nicholas, Natalia, and me up for Salsa lessons at the SSQQ Dance studio. That evening, I gave them the news. Natalia was excited—Nicholas, not so much.

"Mami, are you sure there will be people our age at this class?" Nicholas asked slowly, still trying to be supportive of my new adventure.

"Of course! Everyone wants to dance the Salsa! Don't you watch *Dancing with the Stars*?'

"Natalia and I will go with you this time, but I'm not telling my friends I'm taking a Salsa class with my mom. That's just weird."

"Girls love a guy who can dance! You won't regret it, and it will be fun to do it together," I said rapidly before he could back out.

"Okay, Mom, but if we don't like it, we don't go back," he answered and walked off.

We went to our class on a Thursday evening. The class was in a room with wooden floors, and the teacher was from Panama. The average age of the students was over forty. Nicholas and Natalia looked at each other and then looked at me. They didn't smile for the whole hour. Men and women were separated, and we started with simple steps. Then we were paired up, and we rotated partners every five minutes.

When the class was done, Nicholas and Natalia rushed out to the car. When I arrived, they both shook their heads from side to side.

"Mami, I don't want to go back. It's just a bunch of smelly old men, and I didn't like having to switch and dance with everyone. An old man even stepped on my feet!" Natalia complained, annoyed.

"Was it really that bad?" I asked, smiling, though I knew they had endured an hour of torture. "I had fun. The music was great."

"Mami, it sucked," Nicholas said emphatically. "I don't want to go back either! I got stuck with all the ladies, and they all smiled at me the whole time. Natalia is right. It's just a bunch of old people."

"I don't think they're old. They're all around my age, and they want to dance. You don't have to go back, but I think you'll regret it. You're Latinos; you need to know how to dance the Salsa."

"We'll learn with our friends. Sorry, Mami, but you wasted your money on us. We're not going back, and you better not tell our friends we went with you," Nico said emphatically.

They kept their word. They never went back. Instead, the dance studio gave me an extra free month of classes.

In February 2010, Anne called to invite me to dinner. She had a proposition for me.

"Pam, Karen and I have been thinking we need to set you up on a date, and we have someone we want you to meet."

"Really? Who is it?" I asked, interested.

"He's a Texan—tall, cute, and widowed. He grew up in Houston. I helped him when his wife passed."

"How long has he been widowed?"

"Around a year."

"Is he dating someone right now?" I asked, filled with curiosity.

"I don't think so. Karen said she tried to set him up before, but it didn't work."

"What makes you think he would want to date me? I have an accent, and I didn't grow up in the States. I'm not sure about this; let me think about it. I haven't dated too many Americans. They make me nervous."

"You can think it over. Let's get dinner on Wednesday at the Thai restaurant at Shepherd and Westheimer. Seven o'clock," she said excitedly.

"Okay, it's a deal." I put down the phone and smiling. *I'm happy with my life,* I thought, *but it would be fun to go on a date.*

Wednesday arrived. I was excited to see Anne. Karen, my divorce attorney's daughter, was with her. We sat in a booth, and the conversation began once we'd ordered wine and appetizers.

"I've known him for over a year," Karen said, laughing. "He's fun to be around. Hasn't dated too much since his wife died, but he is ready to meet people. He has a good sense of humor and he's kind."

"Come on, Pam. You need to start going out again," Anne encouraged. "There are good people out there, and you can always call us for support. You might even fall in love."

I looked between the two of them. "You're right. Give him my number."

When I got home that night, I went to Natalia's room.

"Natis, Anne is going to set me up on a blind date. Can you find him on the computer so we can see what he looks like? You know what I'm talking about, right? Where you stalk someone and find out who they are."

Natalia laughed. "Mami, you mean google him? Everybody does it." She pulled her laptop onto her lap. "I'm on it. What's his name? I'll find a picture so we can make sure he's safe and not a creep."

I sat beside her in anticipation. "Mark Livesay."

Time went by as she focused on her laptop. Anticipation made me impatient. I was anxious and excited at the same time.

"So, what have you found, Natis? What does he look like?" I tried to look at the screen.

"I can't find what he looks like or any information about him. That's strange. Usually you can find at least a picture. He must not use social media a lot." She continued to search his name.

I picked up the phone and called Anne. "I'm not too sure I want to go out with him. Natalia can't find anything about him online. Anne, are you sure it's going to be safe?"

"Yes, don't worry. He's nice. Just think of it as meeting a new friend. You might enjoy each other's company and go to the movies or to dinner. Don't think about it too much," she reassured me kindly.

Within the week, I received a phone call.

"Hi, am I speaking to Pam? I'm Mark. I got your number from Karen." His voice was deep and strong; it took me by surprise.

"Hello. They told me you'd be calling." I tried not to sound too excited.

"I'd like to meet you." He sounded confident. "Would you like to go to dinner Friday night?"

"Yes, I don't have plans for Friday night. Do you want to meet me somewhere? I live close to St. Thomas High School," I said, trying to sound casual.

"I'm a gentleman. I'll pick you up. What type of food do you like?"

"I like Italian, and I'm close to La Griglia. It has good food and a nice environment. What do you think?" I asked.

"I believe we have a date. I'll pick you up on Friday at seven. I'll need your address before we hang up."

"Are you ready?" I proceeded to give him my address before putting down the phone. I ran to find Natalia. She was in the living room, wrapped in a blanket and watching TV.

"Natis, I have a blind date on Friday. Pause the movie; I need your help!" I said urgently. "Help me pick out something for Friday."

"Mami, a real date! Let's go." She paused the TV and ran to my room. We separated out several outfits so I would have options. That week, I exercised daily, got a manicure, and asked my coworker who was twenty years younger than me for advice on blind dates.

When Friday finally arrived, I was nervous all day long, but excited. I felt like a teenager. At seven sharp, the doorbell rang. Nicholas opened the door.

"I'm Mark. I'm here to pick up your mother." He shook Nico's hand.

"Nice car," Nicholas commented. "Is it a Corvette?"

"Yes, it's pretty cool. Smooth ride too."

"I like it. Go up the stairs. My sister will call my mom," Nico said casually, still admiring the car. Mark climbed to the second floor, where Natalia was sitting on a barstool, her laptop open in front of her.

"Hi, I'm Natalia. Mami is almost ready. Do you like dogs?"

"Yes, I love dogs. I have a dog named Charlee."

"Oh, good. Tell me about Charlee. My dog is Sofia. She's an Italian greyhound, and we named her Sofia for Sophia Loren. My mom loved that actress, and she loves Italy."

Mark smiled. "Well, Charlee is also unique. We found her at a church called St. Charles Borromeo when she was a puppy. She ran into the church; she wanted to be inside where all the people were. After mass, the usher offered her to us. I have four kids, so they jumped at the idea of having a dog."

"Mami, Mark is here to pick you up," Natalia screamed, getting off the stool and looking up the stairs to the third floor.

I walked down the stairs with butterflies in my stomach, not sure what to expect. From the stairway, I looked at Natalia first and saw her smiling. I said a silent prayer, hoping it would be a nice evening and not one to regret. When I saw him, I smiled. *He is cute. Anne was right!*

"Hi, I'm Mark. Nice to meet you. Are you ready? Natalia and I were just talking about our dogs." He smiled.

"Nice to meet you too. Yes, I'm ready. Thanks for picking me up. Did you have any trouble finding the townhome?"

"No, not at all. I know my way around Houston pretty well. Let's go; we have reservations for seven thirty."

I turned around to say goodbye to Natalia. Nervously, I watched her face carefully for a clue; she was the hawk.

"You look pretty, Mami," she said reassuringly, giving me a smile and a wink.

"Thanks, Natis. I'll be back soon. I love you." More confident, I led the way to the door.

We walked outside, and Mark opened the passenger's door of a black Corvette. I had never been in a sports car before. I sat and had to brace myself; I felt like I was going to fall through the floor. He accelerated, and I held my breath. The car roared. My heart beat fast.

When we arrived at the restaurant, I tried to get out of the car and realized it wasn't that easy. He graciously came around and helped me out. When we stepped into La Griglia, there was an atmosphere of celebration all around. The murals on the walls were vivid colors, the tables were packed, and the waiters were busy going from table to table, taking orders.

I've always loved Italian restaurants. Italians love life, food, and wine. They are loud and charismatic, and they express themselves with both voices and hand gestures. For them, life is carefree, less structured, and disorganized, yet people live and enjoy the moment.

I took a deep breath. I loved the organized chaos.

At the restaurant, we were both nervous. He pulled out my chair for me. I thanked him and smiled, thinking, *He is a gentleman.* He ordered a Chianti, appetizers, and a delicious meal. We talked about our careers, our backgrounds, and our children, and we laughed. We had some similar experiences: our children were in the same age ranges, and we both liked outdoor sports.

The evening was wonderful.

When he took me home, I unlocked the gate that opened onto a small walkway that led to the front door. He walked me to the door, waited patiently while I unlocked the door, and then gave me a small kiss on the cheek. Then I proceeded to walk him back to the gate so I could lock it. To my amazement, he went around the gate on the outside yard and waited for me to go into the townhouse and lock the door.

He would continue this routine for the next couple of years.

Inside, I ran to the family room on the second floor. Nico and Natalia were watching TV, waiting for me.

"Mami, how was your date?" Nicholas asked, smiling. "He has a cool car. Can you date him long enough for him to give me a ride?"

"Mami, did you have fun?" Natalia asked. "He likes dogs. If he likes dogs, he might be okay . . . are you going out again?"

"It was really, really nice. He treated me like a lady. He opened the door for me and pulled out my chair at the restaurant. I couldn't believe it. It was refreshing. He's a widower and has children your age. He loves the water and boating. I hope he calls me again." I smiled as I recounted my evening for them.

"Mami, this is a 'love my life' moment," Natalia said. "Come on, Nico, all together! Mami had a good date with Mark."

We all raised our hands and, laughing, shouted "I love my life."

After saying good night, I headed upstairs to my room. I had a phone call to make before turning in.

"Christy, are you still awake?" I asked excitedly when she picked up the phone.

"Mami, of course. I've been waiting for your phone call! How was it? Where did you go? Did you have fun? Tell me everything."

"Well, he's tall, handsome, and a gentleman. I had a wonderful time. He has a deep voice with an unusual Texas accent." I continued to fill in the details.

"Mami, don't fall for him. Nico called to tell me he has a sports car and that he's in his fifties. He might be having a midlife crisis. You have to be careful." I heard concern in her voice.

I laughed. "It was a wonderful evening. Don't worry."

"Mami, I'm happy it was a good date, but remember, we notice things before you do. If you keep seeing him, I'm going to have to come home to meet him. I need to check him out before you get too involved."

Before going to bed, I prayed, *God, you know I'm a romantic. Please help me not rush into a relationship that is not for me. Give me clarity, Lord. Let your will be done in my life. Protect and guide my children. Amen.*

For the next forty-eight hours, there was silence in my life. Thoughts were running through my head, and I couldn't get him out of my mind. *He seemed so nice. I wonder if he'll call. Maybe I should just shoot him a text; maybe I shouldn't . . .*

I called Anne.

"Anne, do you think he's going to ask me out again? He hasn't called, but I really had a good time."

"Pam, he's probably just as scared of dating as you are. I'll call Karen. She can get him to talk. If you had a good time, that's all that matters. I'll call you later if I hear anything." She was laughing as she said this.

I asked Nico the same question. "Should I text him? Maybe I could just say hi?"

"No, Mami, no. You have to wait. Guys are different. He probably thinks he needs to take it slow so as not to scare you. If he calls you again, remember I would really like to have a ride in that car!" He gave me a reassuring hug before walking away.

On Sunday night, the phone rang. I looked at the number before answering and felt butterflies in my stomach. I was nervous. It felt like the excitement of a teenager. I took a deep breath and answered calmly.

"Hello?"

"Hi, Pam, this is Mark. I have two tickets to the Rodeo on Tuesday night. Would you like to go?" he asked in his deep Texan voice. A smile crossed my face as I took a calming breath, hoping not to sound too excited about the prospect of seeing him again.

"Yes, I get off work around five thirty. Does that work for you?"

"Perfect. I'll pick you up around six fifteen. How was your day?"

We talked for a few minutes about nothing in particular, but it broke the ice. I was excited about the upcoming date. I ran to find the kids, who were playing soccer outside.

"Nico, Natis, I have another date!" I screamed happily.

"Mami, I told you he would call!" Natalia exclaimed.

On Tuesday, I couldn't stop smiling at the clinic. My coworkers were as excited as I was.

That's the beauty of working with compassionate and caring women. They have been silent supporters in my life. Through tears and joy, births and deaths, sharing the human experience of caring for children has brought a deep bond between us.

That evening, I changed several times, piling different outfits on the bed. I regretted not having a pair of cowboy boots, but I had never really wanted them. I wore blue jeans, a teal shirt, and black riding boots. I was a nervous wreck until he picked me up and I saw his beautiful smile.

Brad Paisley was singing that night. I hadn't listened to country music before, but Natalia had made sure that I heard his music Sunday and Monday night. Texas spirit radiated throughout the evening. Boots, hats, cowhides, country music, people smiling, fried Oreo cookies, turkey legs, carnival rides, and laughter were everywhere. Everyone seemed happy, everyone was proud, and everyone was enjoying the Houston Rodeo—the largest in the world.

As the the concert ended, Mark asked, "Do you want to go to the Hideout?"

"The what?" I asked, looking at him curiously.

"Come, I'll show you. They have a band and a small dance hall." He grabbed my hand and led the way there. His touch sent electricity through my body.

When we arrived at the Hideout, I saw people country dancing, going round and round in circles to a two-step tune. I immediately wanted to dance.

"Let's dance," I said, looking into his face.

"Do you know how to country dance?" he asked.

"No, but I'm going to learn with you."

"Okay, then let's give it a try." He led me out onto the dance floor with a smile.

A couple of times, I missed the beat, but he would guide me with his words based on the dance we were in.

"It's a two-step."

"It's a polka."

"It's a little faster."

"This is a waltz; we need to slow down."

Country dancing is similar to a Spanish Pasodoble — double step. If you have a good partner, you can follow.

Mark was an amazing dancer!

We stayed for about two hours and danced the whole time. I fell in love with the music and with country dancing. The songs reminded me of mariachi songs, filled with love stories. We didn't say much on the drive home. We held hands, and the silence was perfect after an evening at the Rodeo.

When we arrived at the townhouse, he looked at me. "Can I see you this weekend?"

"Yes, that would be nice," I responded happily.

"Okay, we'll go buy you some real boots. It will help you glide easier when we're dancing."

He walked me to door and kissed me on the lips. It was a quick peck, but I enjoyed the warmth of his lips.

For our third date on Saturday, he fulfilled his promise. We headed to Cavender's.

"If we're going to go country dancing, you need the right boots," he said after I got in the car.

"Well, nobody can turn that offer down. If I buy boots, when will we go dancing?" I smiled at the thought of another night in his arms.

"Tonight, we'll go to Whiskey River North. You have to have the right music and the right mood. Then the rhythm just flows. I'll be the frame and you'll be the picture, but it's not just on you. We'll be doing this together." He laughed.

"I'd love that. I have a proposition for you. If I learn to country dance, would you be open to taking Salsa lessons together?"

"Who goes Salsa dancing?" he asked curiously, his blue eyes sparkling.

"My whole family and all my Latin friends. You're a good dancer; you can pick it up," I said enthusiastically.

"Can I think about it? That's not really in my comfort zone," he replied nervously.

That evening, when we arrived at Whiskey River, I was in awe. There was sawdust on the floor and cowboy memorabilia all over the place. Toward the back of the room stood a mechanical bull. There was a bride wearing a white dress and a red Texan hat. Her bridal party all wore red dresses with black boots and matching hats. Mark and I laughed at the sight and decided to join them on the dance floor.

We danced, we talked, we laughed.

On the way home, he looked at me and said, "I think I need to learn the Salsa."

I looked at him and smiled.

In the fall, we signed up for Salsa lessons together.

We continued to see each other over the weekends and texted daily. That was, until one day I read, *Can I call you tonight? I'm tired of reading you. I want to hear your voice.* My heart leaped, and I called him right away. After that, the texts got shorter, and the evening conversations got longer.

Two months later, in April, the children invited Father Phil and some friends to come over for a raclette grilling party. I invited Mark, who arrived early. When the doorbell rang later, Mark went to get it. It was Father Phil.

"Hello, Father, it's been a long time!" Mark said, laughing.

"Mark! What are you doing here? Am I at the right house?" Father Phil asked, surprised.

"I believe you are! I'm here all the way from Sugar Land. I haven't seen you much since you left St. Laurence, but when Pam told me you were coming, I wanted to surprise you."

"I didn't realize you knew Pam."

"We went on a blind date two months ago, and I'm still here. God has an amazing sense of humor. I prayed for a nurse because they're compassionate and kind, and I prayed for a woman from the south. God sent me a pediatric nurse who is definitely a woman from the south—she grew up in Colombia but got to Texas as soon as she could." He let out a laugh as he led Father Phil up the stairway.

I was waiting for them both upstairs and grinned at Father Phil before greeting and embracing him. Father Phil smiled. "He's a good man. I'm very happy you both met." It was a powerful statement and a confirmation of what my heart was feeling.

In the middle of dinner, the power went out.

I panicked. "Oh no, oh no! We're in the middle of a party! This can't be happening. We still have a lot of food to cook. All three raclettes have chicken and shrimp on them."

Mark got up to help. "Where did you plug them all in? Which circuit are they on? I'll go check the breaker."

"I plugged them into the wall like I always do. I've never had a problem."

"Do you always use three?"

"No, this is the first time I've used three. There are more kids here today."

He smiled. "I'm here to help. I know about electricity. I'll get this fixed. You just overloaded the circuit, but I can fix it with extension cords. This isn't my first rodeo."

A few minutes later, he'd fixed the issue, and the party continued. After that event, he began to come over with his toolbox, fixing things around the house and helping with their maintenance. It made me feel special that he would help me out in ways I wasn't even aware I needed. One evening, he came with a variety of filters and spent the evening changing air conditioning filters and the refrigerator filter and placing dampers on the light switches to dim the lights.

That summer, the kids and I had the opportunity to go to Machu Picchu for two weeks. It was the first time Mark and I would be apart since we started dating. During the trip, I realized how much he had become part of my life. I missed his presence and his smile. We texted often, but I missed hearing his voice and the sound of his laughter. It was at that point that I truly decided I was ready for a deeper commitment, and I put aside my fears. When I came home, I allowed myself to embrace our relationship fully.

Mark and I dated two years before he asked me to be his wife. In those years, I learned about healthy relationships. I had an opinion and a voice. I mattered. We learned to communicate. We respected each other for who we were and what we believed as individuals while we were becoming a couple. We learned to compromise.

We came from different experiences and we didn't always agree on politics, religion, or social issues, but we learned to listen to each other and accept that we could have different views. We learned boundaries. We laughed together but never made fun of each other. We learned to pray together, to share our personal beliefs and our faith.

I learned to trust him. We both made an effort to balance our work with play so we could spend time together — sometimes on dates, sometimes working silently. I learned he needed space for projects; he learned I needed people and relationships. We learned mutual respect.

On December 29, 2012, we got married. On the right side of the church, Mark stood with his four children beside him, and on the left side, I stood with mine. Father Phil married us at St. Laurence, Mark's previous church. After we pronounced our wedding vows and we were officially man and wife, we faced the crucifix, raised our arms together, and said, "I love my life. Thank you, God."

ACKNOWLEDGMENTS

I want to thank my children who, year after year, read the letters I wrote to them and responded lovingly. They helped me make this book a reality.

I never knew writing was so much work. I want to thank Christina, my daughter, and Scott Douglas for getting me a gift certificate for a writing coach in December 2017. I met my coach, Fern Brady, in April 2018, and she guided me in transforming a diary and letters into a book. Without her constant support and encouragement, this book would not be possible.

I want to thank Dorothy Tinker of D Tinker Editing for copyediting and formatting my book. Thanks to your work, my book has become a polished novel.

I also want to thank all my beta readers: Diana García, Diane Huber, Guillermo and Alejandra Marcos, Angie Wences, Elsa Lopez, Darlene Estrada, Ana Cecilia Gonzalez, Carmen Macossay, Cynthia Adams, my aunt Diane Dixon, and author Johnnie Bernhard. They took the time and effort to read through the manuscript and give me feedback. I couldn't have done it without their help.

Mom, you taught me service and love. Your constant presence in my life gave me courage. I know I have an angel in heaven. Thank you for teaching me to be a mother.

Finally, I want to thank my beloved, Mark, for his constant support and love over the years and for the time to work on this project.

Most importantly, I want to acknowledge God's continual grace in my life.

ABOUT THE AUTHOR

Pamela Lombana is a nurse practitioner living in Houston, Texas. She owns and operates Clinica La Salud LLC in Spring Branch. She is a regular contributor to *Mi Familia* magazine. *Full Circle* is her first full-length publication, a memoir that covers her time dealing with alcoholic relationships. She enjoys writing, traveling, hiking, and creating memories with her family and her husband, Mark.

Made in the USA
Monee, IL
09 March 2020